No Body's Perfect

A helper's guide to promoting positive body image in children and young people

Dr Vivienne Lewis

AUSTRALIANACADEMIC**PRESS**

First published 2016 by:
Australian Academic Press Group Pty. Ltd.
18 Victor Russell Drive
Samford Valley QLD 4520, Australia
www.australianacademicpress.com.au

National Library of Australia Cataloguing-in-Publication entry:

Author:	Vivienne Lewis.
Title:	No body's perfect : A helper's guide to promoting positive body image in children and young people /
ISBN:	9781922117748 (paperback)
	9781922117755 (ebook)
Subjects:	Body image--Psychological aspects.
	Body image.
	Body image--Social aspects.
	Body image in children
	Self-perception in children
Dewey Number:	155.2

Publisher: Stephen May
Copy Editor: Rhonda McPherson
Cover design: Jemima Ung
Page design & typesetting: Australian Academic Press
Printing: Lightning Source

"*No Body's Perfect* is a powerful tool for parents and teachers who seek to understand the complexity of body image and help young people celebrate all their body does for them. The book is full of practical activities to help young people understand body image and develop a healthy scepticism for striving for a certain physical 'ideal'. The book is also a wake-call for adults everywhere that the way we talk about and feel about our own bodies has the power to shape the next generation's body image. Dr Lewis's book is a call-to-action for teachers and parents to lead by example and teach the next generation to love the skin they're in."

Kimberly Gillan, health journalist / Coach health writer

"In *No Body's Perfect* Dr Lewis offers techniques informed by research and clinical practice for use by parents, teachers and others concerned about appearance-related dissatisfaction and distress in children and young people. Practical suggestions for activities and classroom exercises mingle with the voices of young people and parents whose lives have been affected. Guidance includes advice for adults about how to moderate the key factors influencing appearance dissatisfaction, including how adults can be effective role models, how to help young people deal with appearance-related teasing, how to improve their media literacy & suggestions on how to regulate the use of social media. Helpfully, the book addresses the current gap in the literature on body image in boys with the inclusion of a chapter focussing on how to talk about and address body image in boys. This book addresses a key issue for young people in a timely, practical and accessible way."

Professor Nichola Rumsey, Co-Director, Centre for Appearance Research, University of the West of England, Bristol, U.K.

"Over the last decade I have seen enormous cultural and technological pressures continue to impact boys and young men in the areas of identity and body image. When boys and men struggle and are not helped to accept and value themselves they quickly look to external and often damaging stereotypes. In *No Body's Perfect* Vivienne Lewis offers solid, practical and much needed guidance for parents, health workers, policy makers and educators in this important space. She gives us long overdue permission to help boys and men begin a constructive dialogue about body image from which we will all benefit."

Jonathan E Doyle B.Ed (Sec Spec) MLMEd, Director of Choicez MEdia, International Speaker, Author and Educator.

"Dr Lewis has been my daughter's psychologist through her battle with a chronic illness and as she transitioned through positive and difficult stages of her recovery. Dr Lewis has given me the knowledge and support required during the most difficult of times. Her empathy and professional manner have been extremely important and I believe that her book will provide insight and knowledge to many just as she has done for me."

Parent

Contents

This book is dedicated to all those caring for children and young people who want them to grow up being happy and healthy individuals, accepting their bodies and themselves for the beautifully unique people they are. Thank you to all my clients including parents, carers, teachers, counsellors, children and young people who have shared their personal experiences with me and taught me how to strive to be the best body image helper I can be.

— Vivienne

N*o Body's Perfect* is an easy to read guide to promoting positive body image and mental health in children and young people. Each chapter addresses an important area or issue of body image and provides parents, carers, teachers and counsellors (which includes any health professional working with children) with evidence-based strategies for improving body image, mental and physical health in children and young people.

Since an important part of developing and fostering positive body image in children involves being a positive adult role model, this book will also assist you with your own positive body image and mental health.

It is also designed to be used in and out of the school and home environment with children aged six years and up. Highlighted throughout are activities for class or home use that the reader might use in their own work or home setting. There are also direct quotations from parents and children that the author has worked with over the years to provide real-life examples of the issues being discussed.

As well as specific activities, this book also provides teachers and educators with guidelines on how to discuss the topics covered and recommendations for schools on fostering healthy body image and well-being at the school, class and student level. Teachers may choose to take a class through a specific chapter or to go through each chapter as a series covering all aspects of the book. It is also planned that worksheets to assist teachers with the activities in this book as well as further activities will be available soon after publication on the publisher's website **www.aapbooks.com**, under the 'Support Materials' menu.

By the end of this book you and the children and young people you care for will:

- Learn what body image is and the issues involved.

- Learn about your own body image and how to improve it.

- Learn how to be okay with your body and yourself.

- Learn how to be a positive role model to others.

- Learn about teasing and body bashing and how to handle it.

- Learn about the dangers of dieting.

- Learn how to be media literate.

- Learn about eating disorders.

- Learn why and where to go to for help.

- Learn how to foster mental health and healthy living.

CHAPTER 1

What's all the fuss about body image?

> My name is Tom and I'm 15 years old. I never worried about my body until I hit high school. In year 8 I was the shortest and thinnest boy in the school and I knew this because we had a classroom activity where everyone lined up from shortest to tallest. I was even smaller than the shortest girl. I was humiliated and hated the constant teasing. Being called shorty and a girl because of the way I looked. I hit puberty late and so suffered this teasing until finally last year I started growing taller and broader. I'm now no longer the shortest but I still get teased for being 'too thin'. I hate it, it makes me not want to go to school. We had a male footballer come and talk to us boys at school about body image, puberty and mental health. He's one of my favourite sporting heroes. Apparently he was bullied when he was my age and he didn't handle it very well. But he's now so famous and so sporty despite being a bit shorter than his teammates. So he got through it, so maybe I can too?

This chapter starts by defining what body image is, and some of the influences on it, followed by suggestions for classroom and home activities to do with children of all ages. It is recommended that before doing the suggested activities with children and young people, you read Chapter 2 so you understand your own body image and how it may influence your role modelling to those in your care.

Everybody has a body image. It's the *perception* we have of our bodies as well as the *attitudes* and *feelings* we have towards our physical appearance. Some people have a really positive body image and can appreciate and love their bodies and others may have a not so positive image where they dislike their body or think there's something wrong with it. How do you feel about and towards your body? For example, do you like the parts of your body? Do you think it needs changing? What's important to realise is that a person's perception of their body has very little to do with what it actually looks like. This is why you may have a child in your care or person you know whom you think is aesthetically beautiful but they perceive themselves as flawed or ugly. This is also why just telling someone they are beautiful may not resonate with them, particularly if they've thought they were flawed in some way for a long time.

Body image incorporates thoughts or the things you tell yourself about your body, along with the things you believe about physical appearance and what you think you 'should' look like or what you consider is 'acceptable'. The thoughts and beliefs you have about your body and physical appearance generate feelings about your body and yourself. Sometimes people can feel awkward, self-conscious or down because they don't like the way their body looks. This is a negative body image and can lead to feeling unhappy with yourself. People with a positive body image generally feel much more positive about themselves and their life and this is what we're going to work on. Learning to appreciate your body, what it does for you, will lead you to feel more confident and comfortable and feel great about yourself! This will then help you role model positive behaviours and attitudes to the children and young people in your care. Role modelling attention to qualities and traits and speaking well of others and not making comments based on people's appearance can help teach children and young people to value people for who they are, not what they look like. Appreciating the body for what it does too, not how it looks. We'll talk more about this in the chapter on positive role modelling.

The way we feel about our bodies can change from day to day and hour to hour depending on what we're doing, wearing, who we're with, whether we've been physically active or not and what we've eaten. But not feeling good about your body constantly is no good for your health and wellbeing. For children and young people especially, they need to feel good about themselves and that includes their body, otherwise they're more likely to experience mental health concerns that may span into adulthood. That's where adults come in, we are the role models and helpers for our children to maximise the likelihood of a positive self and body image.

Puberty is an especially hard time for some young people. It's really common to feel self-conscious when you're going through puberty as your body is changing and you don't have a lot of control over it. You will remember how you felt going through this stage. For example, you may have the thought, 'My hips are so wide, I am sure everyone in the room is staring at them and thinking I'm fat' or 'my breasts are developing and I feel super self-conscious' and this leads you to have negative feelings towards your body. Or for boys, getting worried about their changing voices and bodies and the effects of their hormones. It can be embarrassing for young people who've hit puberty earlier than their peers or whose peers like to tease them making seemingly 'harmless' jokes. But we know too that body image concerns can occur in younger children, pre-puberty, when they notice differences in their and others bodies. For example, common concerns of younger children can be their weight, their size and shape, their hair, facial features and how they look in clothes. It can be hard for the adults in a child's life to assist them in coping with body changes and so in this book we're going to address the specific ways of helping foster a positive body image in a child or young person. There are specific chapters that address specific issues but in this chapter we'll address some general body image issues and ways to address them as a parent, carer, teacher, counsellor and other major adult influences in a child's life. Let's have a closer look at the impact of body image on children and young people. Understanding the issue will help you role model and communicate better with children and young people regarding body image.

How common are body image concerns?

It's really common for young people to be unhappy with aspects of their appearance. Most will have some issue with their body whether it is a particular part or feature or the body as a whole. Body image doesn't discriminate between genders; both boys and girls can dislike certain parts of their body and be unhappy as a result. There's a specific chapter in this book on working with boys, as sometimes it's better when working with groups, to split genders and work in smaller groups.

Looking at the research, the majority of girls and boys aged 12 to 18 years of age want to change at least one aspect of their physical appearance, with body weight ranking the highest. It's very common, often seen as the norm, for girls especially, to want to be thinner and boys to be lean and muscular. The current 'ideal' bodies portrayed in popular media are lean, toned, tall, clear skinned, with a full head of hair look for both females and males. You can see that if you're going through puberty for example, you're very unlikely to have clear skin, your body is changing at different rates and you can't do much to change your height or build. 'Ideals', the bodies that are portrayed in popular media as most attractive and often connected with wealth and success, are hard to achieve for both genders and people of all ages, not just young people but children, middle aged and older adults. It's estimated that less than one per cent of the population actually are genetically able to look this way. It's hard for girls, for example, going through puberty, where their bodies are becoming more rounded, and for boys, being lean and muscular is very difficult to achieve without substantial emphasis on muscle building activity and specialised dieting. So these idealised images are virtually impossible to achieve without the right genetics, substantial focus on diet and exercise and use of products to change or enhance appearance, not to mention a lot of time and focus on appearance. When it really becomes concerning is when boys and girls start to prioritise body image above other things, such as family, friends, school and career. As well, they can become fixated on 'being healthy' by spending a lot of time on their weight, fitness, and appearance, out of proportion to other things. Whenever a child or young person focuses on one thing at the exclusion of another and they are distressed by this focus or missing out on things, there is reason to be concerned.

Extreme body image concerns

Body image concerns to some degree are almost normal in our society today but when they are extreme a condition called Body Dysmorphic Disorder can be experienced. This is a clinical disorder where a person becomes fixated on a part of their body or feature that they perceive is flawed or defective in some way. This perception is not shared by others and can cause the sufferer enormous distress. The sufferer often spends much of their time repetitively checking this feature and is preoccupied with thoughts about it. For example, a young person may perceive that their eyes are too close together and become obsessed with this, constantly checking and measuring, seeking constant reassurance but unable to be reassured, and becoming extremely distressed by it. This condition occurs in both males and females. The form of this disorder which typically occurs in males is called muscle dysmorphia. This will be discussed in Chapter 4 in regards to boys' body image. If you suspect a child or young person in your care is suffering from this condition, professional help should be sought.

When do body image concerns start and what impact does it have?

Body image concerns can start as soon as children are with others and they start to compare their bodies, which may even be in pre-school. They have also, by this age, been around adults and older children and observed their behaviour and attitudes around food, weight, size and shape. There is a general fear of fatness, for example, starting as soon as children are around others and start to notice differences. It's not uncommon for children in primary school to experience peer pressure to look a certain way. Being 'fat' is a common thing for both girls and boys to be teased about and with rates of overweight and obesity increasing this 'fear of fatness' is becoming a mounting concern. We know, for example, that obese boys and girls have significantly lower self-esteem than their non-obese peers, as they are more likely to be teased for their appearance. This can lead not only to unhappiness with the self, but also engagement in dangerous behaviours such as dieting, over exercising, emotional eating, use of steroids and supplements, spending a lot of money on cosmetics, consideration of plastic surgery and general preoccupation with appearance. In some cases body dissatisfaction can lead some children to develop eating disorders such as anorexia, bulimia, and binge eating disorder.

In terms of the *prevalence* of eating disorders this is hard to judge due to the secrecy and shame associated with eating disorders and accompanying mental health conditions. But it is estimated in Westernised nations (where there is social pressure to meet standards of beauty that include thinness) that between 40% to 60% of boys and girls are unhappy with some aspect of their appearance. Strong body dissatisfaction is certainly apparent in children 12 years and up but you do see body dissatisfaction and even eating disorders in younger children. There is a strong drive for thinness in our society, which is advertised to be achieved through dieting. It is often this dieting that leads to eating disorders. Eating disorders are seen mostly in Western countries but also in non-Westernised counties such as Japan, the Middle East and People's Republic of China, due to the influences of the West. So body image is a very serious issue, one deserving of attention in the home and at school. There is a specific chapter on eating disorders that is important to read to understand the issue more clearly.

We know that adults are at risk of body image dissatisfaction and even eating disorders as they transition through life whether that be through pregnancy, aging, menopause and physical ill health. Anyone with a family history of eating disorders is at greater risk of body dissatisfaction. Also, those engaged in competitive sports and sports emphasising physique (i.e., ballet, gymnastics, dancing, body building, and horse riding) are more susceptible to body image concerns and eating issues. It's important, as an adult, that you understand your own body image and the influences on it. Ask yourself the question of how you feel about your body and why? Understanding yourself will help you promote positive body image in children and young people. Make sure you read the chapter on understanding your own body image and how to help yourself as well as the chapter on the essentials of positive role modelling.

The impact of the importance placed on body image

Why are some people affected by their body image to the point where how they feel about their body affects their day-to-day life and others don't seem to care? A lot lies in the *importance* we place on appearance, weight and shape. For example, if my self-esteem is built on my family and school and they're going well, then I'll feel good; if on the other hand my self-esteem is built on being thin and I perceive that I'm fat, then I won't feel very good at all. This feeling bad will likely lead me to stop doing things that make me feel good because I become preoccupied with my body and appearance thinking that changing my body will lead to greater happiness. In reality, changing the body (i.e., losing weight or building muscle) often results in a short-term increase in body satisfaction but this effect is not lasting and can often turn in to an obsession with appearance to maintain changes or a drive for even more weight loss, toning and body enhancement.

It's important to note that *the way you see your body may not always be the same as others see it*. We can all think of examples where we have given someone a compliment on their appearance only for them to disagree or fob off our compliment. This is an example of a difference in perception. Often when looking in the mirror you may look at your body and see all the things 'wrong' with it. We often over analyse our appearance when we look in the mirror, scrutinising it and looking for flaws. Others generally don't do this when they look at us. Our perception of ourselves is also often distorted, and not a true reflection. It can change depending on things such as our mood, our clothing, the angle of a mirror when our body is on show, how rested or tired we are, what we've eaten, how much exercise we've done, among many, many other factors. So, often what we see in the mirror isn't our true reflection, it's our *perception* of our reflection, and this can change. Our perception can be positive sometimes and negative other times. Think about what influences your perception and try and work on ways to maximise the positive.

We need to try and maximise the positive perception of our bodies and this sometimes involves listening to others. It's quite common, for example, for parents, partners, or friends to comment on how beautiful or attractive we are but we don't think or believe this. We don't see what they see in essence. This is often because those who care about us see us for our qualities and positive elements, they don't scrutinise our bodies like we do. Have a think about times when someone has given you a *complement* on your appearance and you've been surprised. This is an example of how different our perception can be to others. Ask yourself, what would it be like if I saw my body how positive people see it? What would happen if I tried to take on board the complements from others? This is a great activity to do with the children and young people in your care. Ask them to think about their own body image, how do they see themselves and what influences it. What positive feedback have they received? Learning to accept complements is an important part of developing a positive body image. Write down the next compliment you receive and really think about it whether it's about your appearance or not.

> Bringing up three boys and one girl, I've always focused
> on the qualities a person has and why they're a good
> person and communicated this to my children. We talk
> about why someone is a good friend, for example. I try

to stay away from making appearance comments. Of course I will tell my children they are beautiful but this is based on their inner beauty. That attractive people have inner beauty and it doesn't matter what's on the outside. This can be tricky especially when my children come home and tell me about other children being teased for how they look. We talk about respecting everyone whether this be talking about their outer or inner self. My children stand up for others who are being teased and that makes me very proud. — *Helena, mother*

Some general rules for class exercises

Before beginning an exercise on body image it's good to set some ground rules with the group. For example, that everyone respects each other's opinions and contributions, that what's said in the group stays with the group, no laughing or making fun of each other, and the like. It is important students feel safe to contribute their personal experiences.

Sometimes, with certain topics students will start to talk about things which may be unhelpful or even harmful to the group. It is important that you have a 'do no harm' policy and are able to redirect discussions if needed. For example, it's quite common for students to start talking about dieting and what they do to lose weight, gain muscle, etc and some of these discussions may involve harmful practices. In these cases remind students that they're discussing 'helpful' ways to improve body image and feel more positive. There is a chapter on eating disorders and how talking about dieting is harmful and it might be an idea to read this before starting a body image exercise.

Always end on a positive note making sure students know where to go to get help, who they can talk to and what strategies they can use to feel good about themselves. Having the school counsellor or pastoral care person on hand is a good idea especially for those students who may have more serious body image issues including those with eating disorders. Look up the help lines and services in your area that students can access for free and confidential advice and assistance.

For an issue as sensitive as body image it's often a good idea to split the students into genders and smaller groups to stimulate discussion and to make students feel more comfortable sharing.

Stimulating a discussion

Ask your group what they think body image is and how it influences their life. For example, students may say 'it's what your body looks like' and you can correct and say it's actually our *perception* and not usually an accurate picture of what our body looks like. Students will likely say how they *feel* about their body can make them feel good sometimes and not so good other times. Have a discussion around this and make the point about how our perception influences how we feel. Use the introduction to this chapter as a guide to defining body image and correcting misunderstandings as well as the chapter on understanding your own body image.

There are no right or wrong answers so just acknowledge what the students say and thank them for their contribution. Some of the points you'll want to highlight are:

- What is body image?

- How do you feel about your body and why?

- We can chose how we feel about our body.

- What things make you feel good about your body? Some suggestions are, wearing your favourite clothes, being physically active, getting complements, focusing on the function of the body rather than its aesthetics, appreciating other people's bodies, not teasing others for how they look.

- Try and steer students away from making appearance-based comments about others. Ask — what positive comments could you make to your friends as a person to make them feel good? Here you want to stay clear of students commenting that so and so is the prettiest or most handsome of the group and other such appearance based comments.

- What qualities do we like or admire in others? Realise that what we like about others may have nothing to do with what they look like.

- Which adults do they admire and why? (Focus here on qualities not looks.)

- Always finish with an activity about what can they do as individuals to make themselves feel good. Such as have fun with friends, exercise for fun and fitness, play games, do their favourite activity, and so on.

- Remind students about confidentiality of each other's stories but encourage them to discuss what they've learnt at home.

Class Activity: The influence of culture

Our culture is a huge influence on our body image. Have a think about how 'idealised' images are portrayed in the media now and what was valued over history. For example, in war zones and famines, being plump and well nourished was idealised as it was seen as a sign of wealth. In the late 19th century, large bathers were pictured representing the ideal female form and in the 1800s Renoir's paintings depicted a large rounded figure as ideal. Even in the 1940s and 1950s idealised figures like that of Marylyn Monroe were of a curvy figure with little body tone. This is in stark contrast to now where being thin and toned is associated with wealth and fortune. It was in the 1960s where models such as Twiggy became the popular look and then in the 1990s the heroin chic waif-look became popular. These figures are unhealthy and unattainable and had a direct relationship with the increase in females experiencing body dissatisfaction and an increase in eating disorders. For males too, in the 1990s the male figure increasingly became portrayed for his looks rather than the function of his body. More emphasis in advertising was on the semi-naked male body, looking seductive, well groomed, and often shirtless with underwear on and enlarged genital size. Students can see images of men in advertising across the centuries and in the 20th century and see the change.

Body image over the centuries

A topic that often stimulates good discussion is getting students to research the change in body image over the centuries and for different cultures and ethnic groups. You could run a class activity on the history of body image that aims at educating students about how beliefs about the body are different in different cultures and over time (you can Google the history of body image and find images of bodies over the ages to stimulate discussion). This leads nicely into discussion about where our body image beliefs come from. For example, in Westernised societies, those that adopt Western cultures such as Australia, Northern Europe, Northern America (US and Canada) and New Zealand are most affected by negative body image due to the emphasis on appearance in these cultures; in particular, the idealisation of thinness. So we tend to see body image issues mainly in developed countries but also those Eastern countries that are influenced by the West, for example, in their advertising. When we compare our Western culture to cultures that do not have an epidemic of body obsession, such as Eastern or tribal cultures, there are some significant differences. One difference is about worthiness and all people being worthy of respect and dignity. In these Eastern and tribal cultures children are taught that they are born being worthwhile, they don't need to earn it, they don't need to achieve it through their appearance, they already have it, it's innate. They have lessons on being spiritual and connected to one's body and self, being connected to nature and to others spiritually. They have daily rituals that involve prayer, meditation, and dance. Appearance is meaningless to some degree. Many religions focus on this innate worthiness and spirituality and your school will likely have values around this.

Contrasting Western to Eastern cultures is interesting for students to investigate, highlighting that in our Westernised culture, body obsession is rampant and we are largely taught that our worth comes from how we look and how much money and valuables we have, the status of our job, whether we have a family, how many friends we have including 'Facebook likes'. Many children believe that they have to be wealthy, smart, attractive, or athletic in order to feel or be special. For many people in our culture, daily rituals consist of weight loss schemes, exercise regimes and checking email or Facebook. So it's your job, as the adult, to teach that our worth is not wrapped up in our appearance but is made up of many things.

Class Activity: Cultural differences in body acceptance

Unfortunately in our Western society, what's promoted is that 'fat' is 'bad' and 'thin' is 'good', largely due to advertising and the influence of celebrities. Talk to students about the societies where being larger in size is actually admired and highly valued. You could talk about African tribes, for example, where being large in size and considered 'fat' is a status symbol. Being 'fat' is associated with desirability, wealth and a higher likelihood to get married. In these cultures people deliberately try to fatten themselves up to be perceived as more attractive. Ask students to compare this difference to our Westernised body image ideals. How might this change how we think and feel about ourselves? Also, getting students to look at magazines and advertising of plus sized models and how these images might make females feel. Even talking about how certain Eastern cultures have changed with the promotion of Westernised body ideals promoted in their advertising. There are some cultures, for example, that now promote being white as associated with beauty and a push to sell facial whitening products to those with Asian skins. What effect do students think this is having on these cultures?

Class Activity: Changes in fashion

Another example is to look back in time at different fashion trends as these have influenced what is seen as an 'ideal' body. Female students will love researching this. Ask them to research how the portrayal of the 'ideal' body has changed over time and how the look of models has changed. For example, if we look back in time to the 18th and 19th centuries, where what was associated with wealth, success and beauty was a voluptuous, curvy, feminine looking woman. Then a change occurred with the industrial revolution where fad diets, including starving oneself, to attain thinness, became popular and women who ate little were admired for their willpower over eating. In contrast, the previous ideal of a larger, voluptuous, healthy body became a symbol of ugliness, a lack of willpower and weakness. There are many theories on why this change occurred but one theory is that clothing advertisers felt that models who had voluptuous, curvy bodies were a distraction to the buyers of clothes and that buyers were focused on the models' bodies in the clothes rather than the clothes alone. The advertisers and sellers wanted the models' bodies to look more like coat hangers so the clothes would hang off the body and not be 'changed' due to the model's body size and appearance. Basically, they felt that a thinner, straighter body would be less distracting to the clothes. So they began reducing the size of their mannequins and demanding more petite and thin models. This then became the new standard of how women were supposed to look, like coat hangers with little body fat and restrained eating practices. You can also look at fashion changes for males where now the models are thin, tall, pale, clear skinned, toned with a full head of hair.

Questions to ask

- Ask students what they think about these changes over the centuries and cultural differences and how it has impacted on how we feel about our bodies and what we value? Highlight that any focus on appearance at the exclusion of other things makes us obsessed with appearance irrespective of what size and shape is considered 'ideal'. So a focus on larger sizes can be just as detrimental to a focus on smaller sizes if size is value based.

- Ask is this okay? Why and why not? You can talk about how any 'ideal' whether large or small in weight can be perceived as negative, when there's only one 'ideal' what does this mean for those who don't fit this 'ideal?

- What can they do to not just follow along with this trend?

- How can they go against the flow? The students might come up with lots of different ways to not be so influenced by the media and culture and how to promote the value of human beings beyond face value.

- Then what can they do to feel positive about their body in an appearance obsessed culture?

- How can they help each other foster a positive body image?

Class or Home Activity: General self-worth

This is a great activity to do at the end of a lesson on body image as it flips students' attention to what's within. It's an exercise about them as people. Ask — I want you to write down who you are including the things you like, the things you're good at, the people in your life, the friends you have, your talents, you're interests, your beliefs and your aspirations. These are all things that make you unique. You're trying here to get students to focus more on who they are rather than what they look like. Although what they look like does make them unique, it's not the only thing to focus on. As a parent you might like to start by saying the things you think about yourself that make you worthwhile as well as why you think your child is worthwhile. This is a particularly good exercise to foster positive body image but also to help those children and young people who might be struggling with their body image.

Class Activity: Hearing somene else talk about body image

As illustrated in the words at the start of this chapter from Tom, hearing from someone else about their own struggles with body image and what they did to overcome them, often helps bring the message home. Having an adult who the students look up to and admire, such as a celebrity or sporting hero, come and speak in your school can be very beneficial. Your local community mental health educational centres should be able to offer assistance here.

Chapter summary

- The first step in helping children and young people with body image is identifying what it is and how it influences them.

- Understanding the influences on body image can help children and young people understand themselves and their thoughts better.

- Educating children and young people about the history of 'idealised' bodies and the experiences of different cultures can open up a discussion.

- Focusing on the self-worth of each child is important to foster positive mental health and wellbeing.

- Getting adults whom children and young people admire to come and speak about body image can help bring home the right messages.

- Understanding your own body image and where your perceptions come from is important in helping children and young people so have a good read of the next chapter to help yourself.

CHAPTER 2

Understanding your own body image and self help so you can help others

I am a mum of three girls. I grew up disliking my body as I was teased for being overweight as a child. This harsh teasing resulted in me often pretending I was sick so I could stay home from school. I didn't have a very good role model. My mum was always dieting and commenting on people's weight and size. It made me super self-conscious and I dabbled in different diets from time to time to try and change my body. I even developed an eating disorder at one point. When I decided to become a mum, I was determined that my kids were going to have a positive role model in me to maximise the chance of a positive body image. I ditched the continuous dieting and now eat healthy foods for their function in my body. I talk about celebrating diversity in people not just in body size and shape but also race, ethnicity, religion, personality, qualities and values. I talk to my girls about loving their bodies and treating themselves well. We don't talk about dieting or comment on people's weight. My girls are healthy and have a good relationship with food and their bodies.

This chapter focuses on how body image is formed, the influences on it and how, with the intention of being a positive role model to children and young people, you can start to work on your own body image to feel better about yourself so you can help others. There are exercises in this chapter for you to do to work on your own body image and positive sense of self.

We often think that body image issues are an adolescent or young person's concern but body image issues occur in middle aged and older adults too. Men and women in their 70s and 80s have been diagnosed with eating disorders and conditions such as body dysmorphic disorder, an extreme form of body dissatisfaction where a person is fixated on a perceived body flaw. The concerns in older adults tend to be centred on aging and the change in the body. For example, older adults can be distressed by their wrinkles, arthritis in the joints, sagging body parts, thinning hair, loss of youthful looks, and the like. So by no means is body dissatisfaction only a young person's condition. We know that around 80% of older adults are dissatisfied with some part of their body. Yet there are those that embrace their aging and become happier with their bodies and themselves as they age, worrying much less about the body issues they may have had at younger ages. The difference between the two groups is often in the way a person thinks about their body and themselves and we'll address that here. Have a think about yourself and your aging friends and family and how they perceive and talk about their bodies. Addressing and treating body image issues though is similar at all ages and that's what you'll learn about here.

We've talked about what body image is — that it's a perception of our physical selves, what we think we look like, our like or dislike of it as a whole or its parts, what we think needs changing — its our *thoughts* about our bodies. Body image is also about how we *feel* towards our bodies, whether we have positive or negative emotions associated with it. For example, are there certain situations where we feel really self-conscious about our bodies versus feeling really comfortable? Everyone fits somewhere on the continuum from completely happy to completely unhappy about their bodies and this can change from day to day or hour to hour. Where do you fit?

We'll start by looking at the ABCs of body image and working on how we change our behaviour and thoughts to feel better about our bodies and ourselves. As a role model to children and young people it's important we have a positive relationship with our bodies and learning where our body image comes from is one way to do this. It helps us question our current body image and correct children and young people's misperception.

The ABCs of body image

To start understanding our body image we have to be able to distinguish *thoughts* from *feelings,* a common misunderstanding. When we're in a situation, like at a work social function, for example, we can usually recount the way we feel. Perhaps we feel stressed, anxious, self-conscious, or perhaps we feel motivated and excited and are having fun. We may therefore say it is because of the work/social environment that we feel the way we do. However, what actually makes us feel the way we feel is our *thoughts.* This explains why two people can be in the same situation but have completely different experiences. The event is the same but their feelings are different and this is because of their thoughts. Let's use an example. Two workers are at a work social function. Worker One feels incredibly self-conscious thinking that everyone is staring at them, thinking that what they're wearing doesn't suit them and they don't have the right body shape to wear what they have on. Worker Two is having fun focusing on the conversations they're having and the yummy food coming around. The event is the same but they feel differently: 'Why?' because their thoughts are different. Worker One is thinking, 'I look fat and ugly, I have a horrible body', whereas Worker Two is thinking, 'I am happy with myself and having fun at this event'. Worker One is likely to recount the event negatively and maybe leave the party early because they feel self-conscious and are worried about how they look and Worker Two is likely to stay and have fun thinking what a great night they're having.

Using the ABC model, we call the A the *antecedent* (or event), the B is our *beliefs* (or thoughts) and the C is the *consequence* (feelings and behaviour). Most people think A leads to C but in fact it's the B, our *beliefs* and *thoughts*, that lead to *feelings*. In this chapter we will learn about how to change our thoughts and beliefs in order to feel better as well as changing our behaviour. But for now let's focus on the influence of A, the antecedent and its effect on our thinking. How this relates to our educating and helping our children is through challenging their beliefs about themselves and others' bodies to make them behave in healthy ways and feel good about themselves.

A — Antecedents (events) and the development of body image

A negative or positive body image doesn't just happen one day, it takes time to develop and there are many theories about its development. No one factor alone is to blame. We're talking here about our *perception* of our body as a whole (i.e., do we think we weigh the 'right' amount) as well as its different parts (i.e., do I think my facial features look ok). How we think about our body starts developing from a very young age even before we start school. Have a think about some of your early influences including your parents, relatives, the programs you watched as a child, who you played with. This will have formed our initial body image, which then develops over time and with experience. Our experiences throughout life help shape the formation of our beliefs and thoughts about our bodies and ourselves. If you're a parent or carer you must not blame yourself for your child's anxiety around their body, there are many influences and you will learn how to influence your child in positive ways from now on.

Let's go through a few influences now. Understanding where your body image perception comes from, how it developed, and what's maintaining it, will help you understand your and the children and young people's in your care, current body image. When we can understand our own body image, how it developed and what's perhaps maintaining our beliefs and the way we feel, we're much better able to change it. Knowledge and insight helps us understand ourselves and make positive change if we need it.

Adolescence especially is a time when body image becomes very important and even more important than other things in life. They can become obsessed with what they wear, their body size and shape, comments from others and wanting to look a certain way. Adolescents can spend a lot of time 'getting ready', often much to the irritation of parents and carers. It's normal for adolescents to have some concerns but these should not be out of proportion to other things they're doing or at the expense of having fun, being healthy and happy. If you're concerned, talk to them and seek help.

How much our body image affects our daily life depends on many factors, including how important our body image is to us. Now's a good time to evaluate how much importance you place on your body image. Think of all the things in your life and what you're doing and place body image within them. The importance a person places on appearance and the context in which the body is seen often determine how much their body image affects their life. Ask yourself, how important is it to change the way you feel about your body and behave as a result, to feel better about yourself?

Personal Activity
Think about how much importance you place on your own body image. Why do you place this much importance on it? Is this helpful? Or do you need to try and reduce the importance you place on your appearance in order to feel better? Understanding your body image and its development will help you to make positive changes. You might like to set yourself some positive goals around body image such as 'I want to focus on what I like about my body, not what I don't', 'I want to speak more positively about others' bodies', 'I want to focus less on what my body looks like and more on what my body can do'. Everyone can benefit from a more positive body image.

The influence of the West

There are certain cultural body ideals (i.e., the way the media portrays beauty and attractiveness) that exist in all cultures. In our Westernised society, what is deemed as 'attractive' for male and female bodies surrounds us in multimedia and influences our perception of what boys and girls and men and women should look like and what is 'acceptable' and not. What is deemed 'acceptable' is often very narrow. The way the human body is portrayed in popular media, gives us a point of comparison for our own body. It is this comparison that often leads us to feel positive or negative towards our body. Can you remember when you were growing up what you watched or read and how this influenced your body image? Typically, if we compare ourselves to an 'ideal' (what the media says is beautiful) image, then we're much more likely to think of our body in negative terms in comparison as most people don't look like the images that are portrayed. For example, in Western society today there is a tendency to highly value thinness in women, seeing a thin woman is associated often with success, attractiveness, and better at attracting partnership, attention and wealth. And for men, this ideal image is a lean and muscular figure, characterised as leading to the attraction of women, wealth, health, success and pride. Both 'ideals' (what society says is most attractive) are almost impossible for most people to achieve, yet we are bombarded every day with images of film stars and fashion models that are often dangerously thin and we are fed a message that thin is beautiful or that a real man should be lean and full of muscles.

These images are often accompanied by suggestions as to how we can obtain these bodies too such as through dieting (notice all the fads that are advertised), exercise (often types we have to pay for), use of cosmetic products (that are usually expensive) and even use of drugs (that can be dangerous to our health and mental state). A person can spend a lot of money and energy on trying to achieve these 'idealised' images, usually with little success. These media images also centre on youthfulness so as we age we move further and further away from these ideals which can lead us to feel unhappy as we age naturally. Being realistic about making comparisons to these images is important. There's no point trying to look much younger than we actually are. We might be able to look more youthful, but if we're in our 40s, for example, comparing ourselves to a late teen image is only going to make us feel dissatisfied with our appearance in comparison. Some people will go to great expense and pain, using cosmetic procedures for example, to try and change their body to make it look more youthful. Of course, taking pride in your appearance is normal, but remember to question the extent to which you go. Is this healthy for you?

How do we stop the comparison?

So how do we stop being influenced by these media images? In essence we need to realise that real bodies don't look anything like what is portrayed in the media. For example, in magazines and on the Internet, the images we see are not the true person at all but rather an airbrushed, computer enhanced, touched-up version of the person with no noticeable imperfections. We can certainly appreciate beauty, but realise that it comes in many shapes and sizes. Adolescents, for example, can become very unhappy with the appearance of their skin as they see images around them of clear, unblemished, young looking skin and think that this is normal. Then, as a result, feel ugly or shameful about their appearance and may avoid social situations and school because they are overly self-conscious. Understanding media images, often called *media literacy*, will help you to stop comparing yourself to unrealistic images in the media. Knowing that these images are unrealistic and unachievable will help you to stop aspiring to look like them. In a subsequent chapter, we'll talk about how you can help children and young people be media literate and challenge 'idealised' images.

Celebrating our age, our maturity, our growth of knowledge and wisdom as we get older is another way to not fall victim to trying to move our bodies in line with idealised images. Being happy with oneself is about celebrating the years we have and appreciating ourselves at any age and stage of life. And if we do this in plain view of the children and young people in our lives it will help foster a more positive body image for them.

Personal Activity

Ask yourself: What are the things I read or watch that lead me to sometimes feel negative about my body? Do I need to change or stop bombarding myself with those negative influences? As a family are there things we can do differently at home in terms of what we watch? (You'll learn more about this in subsequent chapters.)
There's nothing wrong with doing things that make your body feel

nice, but always ask yourself, does this make me feel good or does it feed my anxiety and make me more self-conscious?

Western society ideals of beauty are unrealistic and for most of us, unachievable. We may not be able to change the way 'ideal' bodies are portrayed in society but we can choose, as an individual and family, whether we buy into these images or not. One way to not fall victim to media and societal pressure is to challenge these media images and the value placed on looks. Question what you view and encourage the children and young people in your care to do the same. Perhaps you could start looking at people differently too. Look out for the qualities and non-appearance-related attributes that you like in someone. The more you practise doing this with others, the easier it will be to do this with yourself and with your children.

Class or Home Activity: Understanding outside influences

An activity to help understand outside influences on body image is to think about what the outside perceptions or pressures of female/male ideals might be and then think how it makes you feel about yourself given this pressure. Then think about how you would like females/males to be seen in society. What would be valued by society and then how would you feel about yourself if society valued you in this different way? Societal change only comes from us challenging perceptions and values. This is a great activity for teachers to do with children and young people to teach them about questioning media images.

> I ask my kids about the shows they're watching and why they like the characters they do. I try to focus their attention on the qualities of a particular character rather than their appearance. This is hard. My daughter, who is six, loves a particular character because she's beautiful in appearance, gets the prince and lives happily ever after. It's hard to challenge that, so I read her stories at night about characters who are strong in will, have friends, do what they love, stand up for themselves, and are happy as a result. I also talk about the people we know who we admire because of who they are. My daughter says she

loves granny because she gives the best cuddles with her strong arms. — *Michael, father of two girls*

A — The influence of others

Family

Particularly in our early life, our family and the people coming in and out of our household can have a significant impact on our body image. What they say to us and to each other is heard by children and young people. When physical appearance is seen as important including 'being attractive' physically, losing weight, being toned, or eating the 'right foods' for weight management, this can often create a negative body image. Watching a parent or sibling constantly complain about their looks and weight, for example, can have an impact on how much emphasis we place on the importance of physical appearance. Even how children are dressed by adults and what they say about their appearance has an effect. Hearing our mother call herself 'ugly' or 'fat' and needing to lose weight can make us grow up thinking that fat is bad and that we should be focusing on our weight. We can learn from our parents and carers about our relationships with food, such as seeing our parents dieting and not eating certain foods can set up food rules for us about 'good' and 'bad' foods, often leading us to feel guilty if we eat them. Where we've been taught certain food rules as children, we can often carry these through into adulthood. For example, often adults with eating disorders can trace back to childhood where there were certain unhealthy food rules. It can be good to reflect here about the foods you do and don't eat and why. Then ask yourself whether this is relevant and healthy for you now? Sometimes fussy adult eaters can have developed food aversions as children and carry this through to adulthood. When there are behaviours we engage in that are unhelpful or prohibit us from enjoying life, we may have to challenge our food rules and experiment with breaking them.

Teasing

Sometimes men and women can become overly concerned with the way they look as adults because they've been teased about their appearance as children. The most common comments are about being underweight or overweight but comments can also be about facial features, ears, hair, and other parts of the body. We can probably all recall relatives making comments about our weight for example. Constant comments about weight, size and shape by others can lead to a negative body image (as the body becomes the focus of attention) and engagement in harmful behaviours to try and change the body, feeling that only through change, will happiness be achieved. For example, comments from peers about being scrawny or weedy can lead males to feel very unhappy with their appearance and also lead some to feel less masculine or effective as a man. Constant comments from relatives about our bodies, even positive comments, can have a lasting negative effect. It draws attention to the body as a significant source of evaluation about the self. Our appearance is only one part of us but it can be perceived as the only thing people notice and that can make us unhappy. There are examples of women who've always been told how beautiful they are who feel they have nothing else to offer anyone other than their looks. This affects their self-esteem and can lead to great unhappiness. Focusing on a range of qualities, other than appearance, in yourself and others, helps appearance be much less of a focus.

The main way to overcome our adult negative body image is to work out what started this perception and then ask ourselves is this valid or relevant to us now? We can often be holding on to teasing for example, from years back. When we challenge our thinking it's called *disputing our thoughts* through *looking for evidence* against our way of thinking or finding healthier ways to view ourselves.

Personal Activity

Think about where your perceptions of your body and self come from and ask — is this true? What's the evidence for and against? We can often find lots of evidence that supports our perception that there's something wrong with our appearance if we want to, but if you look at yourself through the eyes of those who love and care about you, you usually see a much more positive view. Ask yourself — how can you dispute your negative thoughts to make yourself feel better?

Sometimes there are things that are true about us. We may be a bit overweight, short, bald, funny looking, and so on. We may not be able to change our appearance but we can change how we think and feel towards it. Ask yourself if it is helpful for you to keep on saying negative things to yourself? What is something you can say that is more helpful and makes you feel better? You might say, 'I look how I look and I can't change that, but I choose not to let that make me feel bad about myself'; 'I am a good person, I have talents and people that love me in my life'. Practise challenging your thinking and coming up with helpful and healthy ways of thinking. As well, you might need to distance yourself from negative or appearance obsessed people in your life.

A — The influence of personality: Perfectionism

One personality trait that is often related to poor body image and eating issues is perfectionism, striving to be the very best you can at something, often at the expense of your health and happiness. Those that are perfectionistic have to have things 'just right' and are often difficult to satisfy. So in terms of body image, the person can never be 'enough' — never attractive enough, thin enough, muscular enough, and so on. This comes through as a relentless drive for perfection with the body. Adolescents who are perfectionistic, for example, can be completely consumed by being the 'perfect' weight or having the 'perfect' skin before leaving the house, and are never happy enough with any weight loss goal achievement or body enhancement, always striving to be better. Of course, perfectionism can occur in any domain such as work, study, relationships, family and home. In addressing your perfectionism, it is about reassessing your high standards and asking yourself at what expense does this drive for perfection come at and what other more healthy and happy things could you work towards? This will help you if you have a child who is perfectionistic.

Personal Activity

An activity to do is to ask yourself — what standards do I set for myself and are they realistic? If I don't expect others to live up to these standards, then why do I expect myself to live up to these standards? Is it my perfectionism that's getting in the way of my happiness with my body? How can I accept myself as I am and even love my perceived imperfections?

If you have high standards of beauty, perhaps reassessing these for their merit is important for your own improved body image. Remember that when role modelling to children and young people, they often take on our way of thinking about beauty and people's bodies. So if your standards are high, theirs will likely be too, and they may not choose the healthiest ways to do this.

A – Low self-esteem

Having low self-esteem or undervaluing yourself is connected to poor body image. People with low self-esteem typically never think they're good enough whether this be about appearance or something else. They are hard on themselves and rarely see successes as positive. This low self-esteem as an adult has often developed over time from childhood and adolescence. It may be due to teasing, put-downs from others, mental health issues, parental neglect or abuse, or repeated disappointment. Low self-esteem can lead to depression and anxiety and other mental health concerns and needs to be taken seriously. If you suffer from low self-esteem, getting professional help is recommended.

In contrast, those with high self-esteem, have a positive body image. This is usually due to having positive peer influences and people in their lives that treat them with respect and dignity. So as a carer of children and young people, you can help them learn how to have positive interactions with others such as learning to listen, learning not to judge, and learning to be assertive and standing up for oneself and one's friends.

Personal Activity

Ask yourself — what is your body image like now? How positive or negative is it and why? What's the reason? Then ask yourself what you can do now to turn that around? For example, if you've been bullied in the past, ask yourself, what do people say about me now? What sort of person are you? What can you do to make yourself feel better about your body and self every day without changing your looks? For example, would getting more sleep, hanging around positive people, doing some exercise, having more time to relax, and so on, make you feel better? Don't let things that have happened in the past continue to negatively affect you and if they do, seek help.

B — Beliefs and thoughts

Our perception of our body can be triggered in everyday situations through our daily activities, including our interactions with others. We may find ourselves in situations (events) that lead to the activation of our negative body image thoughts and beliefs (which we've developed as a consequence of our past). We can be seemingly having a good day and then something happens and we feel bad all of a sudden. Take the example of where you might catch a glimpse of your reflection in the mirror and you don't like what you see. You may become distressed and start to feel bad about yourself thinking you're ugly. In order to stop this we need to work on understanding our triggers, questioning our beliefs about ourselves and replacing them with helpful and happier ways of viewing ourselves and our lives. For example, if there are situations or people that make you feel negative about your body and self, then you may need to limit your contact with these people or learn strategies for handling these situations, such as being *assertive*. Being *assertive* means stating what the comment or behaviour is you don't like and that you want the person to stop. This can be quite effective if you're in contact with people who constantly comment about your body or teasing you might receive from friends or family. It is okay to tell someone to stop.

It's not the event that triggers the feeling but our thoughts and beliefs about the event. So if someone teases us it might not impact us if we don't believe what the person is saying. However, if someone makes a negative appearance comment, and our appearance is important to us, we will be negatively affected, particularly if it is repeated teasing behaviour. Our negative thoughts about our appearance (or other aspects of ourselves) have usually been developing over years, not just from one experience, and so have become automatic ways of thinking. So we might not even be aware of our negative thinking because it's occurring quickly and unconsciously. If we can slow this process down though, and become more conscious of it, we're much better able to control and change it. Being aware of our negative self-talk allows us to work on changing it to be more balanced and positive. So catch yourself and think what would be a more helpful way of thinking about this event. For example, if a relative says something negative about your body ask yourself whether this is actually true? Does it matter? And does this comment reflect on you or the other person? Making negative comments about others says more about the person saying it than it does about the person receiving the comment.

When we have negative or unhelpful thoughts, they make us feel bad and often encourage engagement in unhelpful or unhealthy behaviours. What are some of the repeated negative thoughts you say to yourself? Catch yourself thinking negatively, write the thoughts down, and challenge them. How can you speak more positively to yourself about anything including your appearance?

Many of us have what we call *appearance assumptions* or *beliefs* about ours and others' bodies and how they should look. For example, 'beautiful people are always thin', 'an attractive man is someone who is young and muscular', 'I should be on a diet', 'people will only like me if I'm attractive' and the like. These beliefs can lead us to feel bad about ourselves. What beliefs do you hold about appearance that are unhelpful and how can you challenge these? Many of these beliefs are well and truly ingrained in our view of the world. Don't just accept them as truth, challenge your thoughts and come up with more helpful ways of seeing the world. For example, if I instead believe that everyone is beautiful in their own special way including myself, how do I feel?

Personal Activity

Ask yourself — what does my self-talk (thoughts) look like? Is it mostly negative or positive? Is this thinking helpful or harmful? Do I need to challenge my thoughts? This challenging can be through changing your behaviour as well as looking for the evidence or disputing your negative thinking. Challenging and disputing our unhelpful beliefs is important in changing our body image. It's not easy, but it's the way to develop a healthy body image. It's also something we can do with children and young people when they talk negatively about their bodies or others' bodies. Ask them, what's a healthier or more helpful way of thinking about your body? Lead by example and talk about how you challenge your beliefs about your and others' bodies.

> I try to think that everyone is blessed with some special talent or way of being. This helps me look out for the inner beauty in others. When my friends talk about people being 'ugy' I remind them that this is ugliness, looking for the bad in others. I have lost a few peers as a consequence of the way I see the world, but these are not my friends, my friends are those who can see the world through my eyes too and appreciate others for who they are, not what they look like. It helps that my school promotes diversity and celebrating uniqueness. — Monica, high schooler, age 14

C — Consequences — feelings and behaviours

The consequences of *thinking* negatively about our bodies is that we *feel* negative. Depression, anxiety and stress are common ways we feel when we think badly about our bodies especially if our appearance is important to us. When have you caught yourself feeling bad or doing something unhealthy as a consequence of body dissatisfaction? Having a day or two here and there where we feel down is normal, but ongoing negativity is no good. There are people who seemingly don't care about their appearance and seem unaffected by comments or adhering to 'beauty standards'. For these people, other things are more important. So ask yourself — what else could I focus on that would make me feel more positive about myself rather than my body all the time?

When we feel negative about our bodies and selves we're less likely to engage in positive behaviours. Often people with poor body image are more likely to comfort or binge eat, not exercise, avoid situations where their body is on show, use drugs and alcohol to cope, among other unhealthy behaviours. We all have bad days and you know you often isolate yourself or do things which in the longer term aren't very helpful when feeling low. People with ongoing body image issues can do lots of things that reinforce their poor perception of themselves like punishing themselves through dieting or taking drugs, and this just makes things worse.

Ask yourself — when I feel down about my body what do I do? Is this helpful or not? What could I do that would be more helpful? For example, you could go for a walk, do something you enjoy, be around those who love you, speak to yourself kindly and get help, in order to feel better. Knowing what works for you will help you to help the children and young people in your life as they will see you engaging in helpful behaviours when you're down about your body or self.

When you behave in healthy ways this makes you feel better and the better you feel, the more helpful thoughts you will have about yourself. So focus on positive behaviours and being around positive people to make you feel the best you can.

Chapter summary

- Body image develops over time and in response to the experiences and influences in our lives. These influences can be positive and negative.

- The way you feel towards your body is influenced by your thinking, what you tell yourself.

- When you speak kindly to yourself and treat yourself well, you will feel more positive about your body and self.

- Accept what you can't change.

- Be assertive around those who body tease or shame.

- Appreciate your body for what it can do and engage in behaviours that make you feel your best.

- Understanding your own body image and how it was formed will help you better understand where children and young people are coming from and how to help.

- Always seek help if you need it.

Resource

For more self-help for dealing with your own body image concerns it is useful to read my book, *Positive Bodies: Loving The Skin You're In,* published by Australian Academic Press for more specific help on overcoming your own body image issues.

CHAPTER 3

The essentials of positive role modelling

'Mummy is eating cake bad? Should I stop too?' My son asked me this after his seventh birthday party when I refused to eat a slice of birthday cake stating I was on a diet and was trying to lose weight. I didn't realise my son was watching me and my eating and that it was making him question his eating. I now eat a variety of healthy foods with treats every now and then including birthdays. Knowing my son is attending to what I do, I know that I need to be modelling the right behaviours. — *Annabel, 32*

We have already talked about what body image is and how early it is formed and that parents and carers of small children have the biggest influence on their early body image development. This is because, before children start interacting with peers, they watch and learn from the adults in their life. They learn many things from adults as role models, such as feeding themselves, dressing themselves, how to play, how to show emotions, how to be kind, as well as their thoughts about their bodies. They listen to the comments we make about their, our, and others bodies. We have a very powerful influence and we want this to be as positive as possible so in this chapter we're going to go through how, as a parent and carer of young children, you foster a positive body image. Then as children grow older and attend school, their peers and teachers become influential too. For teachers, watching children learn and grow is wonderful and we want them to be healthy and happy. We're there to help them learn about friendships, how to play with others, how to learn, and we keep them safe. Then as children move on to become adolescents, as parents, carers and educators, we try to help them manage puberty, the stresses of academic demands, physical changes to the body, learning about relationships, safe behaviours, and positive mental health and wellbeing. Children and young people look to us, as adults, for guidance not just in what we say to the answers to their questions, but also in the conversations they witness us having with others and the way we talk about ourselves. Being a positive role model to children and young people is not easy especially in a world where there are many influences out of our control (i.e., social media, advertising, peers). But what we can do is try our hardest to be the best role model possible and this is what we'll learn about here.

As a quick overview, the way we be the best role models, as well as educating children and young people about how to be safe in the world, is by doing the following. (All of these tips are addressed in this book in different chapters.)

- Speak positively about others, including their bodies, emphasising more the importance of qualities and values.

- Talk about our own bodies in positive ways as well as highlighting our strengths.

- Teach children and young people about healthy eating for its function in the body.

- Encourage children and young people to be physically active and exercise for fun and fitness.

- Warn them about the dangers of dieting.

- Stand up for children and young people that are being bullied.

- Create safe classrooms free from teasing.

- Educate children about mental health and help seeking.

- Address your own body image issues and get help if you need it.

- Educate yourself about warning signs for disordered eating and mental health concerns.

- Engage them in activities that help them challenge media messages.

- Celebrate children and young people's successes and support 'doing their best'.

- Be open for children and young people to come to you for help. Listen non-judgementally and try and help solve the problem.

- Complement yourself on your efforts with children and young people.

Positive role modelling for young children pre-school

Before children start going to school or daycare, adults in the home, as well as siblings and relatives, play a big part in their development in all areas of life. This includes physical, cognitive, social, emotional, and spiritual development. You want to make this as balanced as possible, so that no one thing is focused on at the exclusion of another. This means providing a child in your care with healthy options for their body and mind including body image.

Children learn about food through us. They will eat what we provide, so provide healthy nutritious foods, but also 'treats' for special times. Talk about food in terms of its *function* in the body rather than 'good' food vs 'bad' food labels. For example, eating fruits and vegetables helps give us energy to run around and play. Protein helps us build muscles so we can run fast and lift things like our bodies up into tree houses. Breads and cereals help fill us up so we can think and sleep well. A little bit of fat in our diet helps our brains work.

Be mindful of what you're eating and drinking as children will copy and ask questions. If you're dieting, make sure you're prepared to answer questions such as why you're eating what you're eating or not. Sometimes talking to children about the different needs of children vs adults can be helpful. For example, adults have stopped growing and are less active so don't need as much energy from the foods they eat. Also, adults need to do more 'structured' exercise as they don't run around and play like children do. This helps children under-stand why you might do more structured physical activity like going to the gym or walking. Making your family an active one where you all get out and enjoy the fresh air, playing sport and games, will encourage your children to do more of this. This is especially necessary if your child isn't naturally active. Remember, children copy what we do so if we are sedentary and constantly using devices instead of moving our bodies and engaging face to face with people, it is likely that your child will become overweight and unhealthy and we know that overweight children are more likely to become over-weight adolescents and adults which creates long term health risks. Overweight children are also more likely to be teased by their peers. So be as active and engaged as you can.

Your child may be a fussy eater for sensory reasons or have had negative experiences with certain foods. Encourage eating a variety of foods rather than giving in to fussy eating. This will stop future eating issues.

Protect your child from the negative influences of others such as those who make negative appearance comments or who tease. If you have people coming into the home that make comments about people's weight, shape or size, talk to them about your family being a body image friendly family where you don't make appearance comments. You choose the rules in your home remember. Your child may be upset by others' comments so be open to talking to them about this.

Be aware of what your young child is watching, listening to and reading and think about its appropriateness. Choose body image friendly books and TV shows (i.e., those that focus on diversity) and talk to them about what they understand from what they watch (often called *media literacy* and is addressed in Chapter 5). As children get older you will have less control as they use social media and electronic devices. Be aware of the parental controls that are on devices so you can monitor your child's exposure to negative media messages whether these be about body image or something else.

Make sure your child is getting enough sleep so they have energy to play and run around to keep their bodies healthy. Make sure you too are looking after yourself with time out for relaxation, social time with friends, quality relationship time, time to look after your spiritual self, as well as managing the stresses of day to day life. Bringing up happy and healthy children requires work so make sure your needs are being met too. Get professional help if you need it.

> I have suffered from depression throughout my life and didn't cope with it very well whilst growing up. My mother had anxiety and depression and my dad was

alcohol addicted. They weren't very good role models as my mum spent a lot of time in bed and dad seemed to drink to 'cope' with stress. When I had my children I decided I wanted them to be as resilient as possible and that started with me. When I feel down I tell my children that 'I'm not feeling my best today' and try to do things that make me feel better. For example I say, 'I'm going for a walk to clear my head' or 'I'm going to call a friend for a chat to talk through the problem'. I've noticed my kids have followed, so when they are having a difficult time we talk about it and try to come up with a solution. Sometimes they just need a hug and other times we need to come up with some strategies to manage. — *Maria, 40*

Personal Activity

Ask yourself — what behaviours or talk do I need to change in order to model more appropriate positive body image to my child? and how will I do this?' Come up with the specifics of what you need to change, how you'll change, how you'll know you've changed and the rewards. You may like to do this on an individual and a family basis. What do we need to do differently as a family?

Positive role modelling for school-aged children

When children start school their peers and teachers become some of the main influences in their lives. But it's important for parents and carers to assist children in developing ways to positively interact with others, respect adults, follow rules, know who to go to for help, manage teasing, manage the media, among many, many, things. Teachers are fantastic at modelling to children respect for others, how to be healthy at school with food and exercise, how to have fun, how to learn, and how to ask for help, just to name a few.

The school environment though can be a significant time for body image issues to begin as children interact with peers who may be unkind or hear adults talking about diets and weight loss. Following are some important points for fostering positive body image in school aged children.

Children will naturally compare themselves to others. So talk about diversity and uniqueness and that nobody is exactly the same and this is what makes everyone interesting. Encourage children to think about differences and the positives of this. Look at the body for its function rather than its aesthetics. A great classroom activity is for children to draw their body and identify each part and what it helps them do and what makes them unique. For example, my blue eyes are from mum, my smile makes other people feel happy, my legs help me run around the playground, and so on. Counsellors can also do this with children on a one on one basis.

Children listen to adults and their peers talking, including their appearance conversations both in the home and at school. 'Fat Talk' in particular, is quite common for people of all ages to engage in and can have a negative impact. Fat Talk is where adults' or peers' conversation focuses on weight concerns and body shape complaints. This commonly occurs by adults when they think children aren't listening. Hearing such talk can lead children to start worrying about their own body weight, shape and size and can contribute to body dissatisfaction. It's important to realise that both talking about underweight and overweight can have negative effects so try to stop having conversations with others about weight and shape and instead model body acceptance and healthy talk. Make your home and workplace environments where healthy discussions take place. Focusing discussions about qualities and attributes is much healthier then conversations about appearance. Never put someone down in front of children because of the way they look. If you're a teacher, and hear peers talking this way, you need to remind them that this isn't the sort of talk we do at school. That we treat people with respect. A class activity on treating each other well and speaking well of others will assist here.

Teasing by peers about the body may start in primary school. In fact, the majority of children will be teased for something with 25% to 30% being teased about their weight. This teasing can lead children to start dieting, overeating or engaging in other unhealthy practices as a result, not to mention feeling sad, anxious, self-conscious, and depressed about themselves. So make your school a no-tolerance to teasing school. There is more on this in Chapter 7 specifically addressing teasing and bullying.

> We take teasing very seriously in our school and have a 'no tolerance' policy for bullying and harassment. Even as staff we are very mindful to speak encouragingly to each other, offer compliments, and keep conversations about diets and body woes to a minimum. We practise what we preach by talking positively about our bodies and ourselves. It's hard sometimes, but as a team, we're encouraging of each other. — *Hilde, primary school teacher*

Personal Activity for teachers

Ask yourself: What does your school do to promote positive body image? How can you, as a teacher, promote positive body image amongst your class? What do you need to be aware of in your own behaviour to ensure you're a positive role model to the children in your care?

> In my high school I see a lot of body bashing going on in the playground with adolescents teasing each other over their weight, shape, height, puberty and in the process see young people becoming quite distressed over this. We have some girls with eating disorders and they can be teased for being 'too thin' or not eating, making them very self-conscious. I have, on occasions, found girls crying in the toilets over this. So in my classes I talk about respecting each other, treating each other well, being supportive and not unkind. Our school also sends

out information to parents and carers about how they
can help their children too. — *Sandra, high school teacher*

If you're a teacher, make your class an active one where you encourage play and physical activity. Children need to be physically active for at least an hour a day to keep their bodies healthy. During breaks, encourage sport and outdoor activities. For parents, encouraging your child to do sport outside of school such as joining a team or doing a fun sport. There are schools that have stand-up/sit-down desks, for example, to help keep children's bodies active during the day so they're not sitting all day. As well, having fruit breaks and the canteen providing a range of healthy snacks and meals. Encourage staff to be active too, so children see teachers and support staff walking around at lunchtime or during breaks; and playing with children and getting involved in their sports. Remember, we're role modelling the behaviour we want children to follow, so if we're active, they will be too.

Minimise screen time at school and at home so children are more active and it will also help with muscle and bone development, eye strain and general physical health. Children will watch us, so if we're always using our devices, they will think this is normal and that they should be doing this too. At home and school, encourage reading books, and making up stories, rather than screen time.

Not all kids love playing sport and some are extremely self-conscious. I try to encourage all kids to play sport and run around at break time. It's good for their bodies and minds. I believe that there's a sport out there for every kid whether it be trampolining, team sports, walking their dog, or playing tag. — *Matt, high school teacher*

It's important for parents, carers and teacher to listen to children and young people's concerns about body shape and appearance. Accept them as valid concerns rather than dismissing them as silly. But help them refocus on other meaningful areas of their life. Don't tolerate peer teasing about weight, body shape or looks. In your home or school, place less value on appearance and more on health and personality, as this promotes positive self-esteem. Lastly, make children feel that they are an important person in the family and class and that they make valuable contributions. You might like to highlight what they do for others including siblings, parents, peers, or the school.

Positive role modelling for young people

As above, the same applies for promoting positive body image in young people at school age. As we discuss in Chapter 6 on puberty, adolescence is a particularly tricky time for body image as their bodies are changing rapidly, often in ways that they don't like. Educating children about the changes to expect is important as well as helping them form their identity in positive ways. Mental health first aid (looking after your emotional self) is important as is teaching young people how to safely manage the media and cyberspace. It is also important to teach children how to deal with emotions as they rollercoaster their way through becoming adults. Here's an example of a classroom activity.

Class Activity: Dealing with emotions

A great classroom activity for dealing with emotions might be to get the class to brainstorm all the ways they can feel better and deal with emotions. So encourage the class to come up with strategies that make them feel good like doing things they enjoy, playing sport, talking to someone, playing music, doing a hobby, and so on. Write up all their suggestions or ask the children to do something creative like drawing all the feelings with pictures of 'helping' behaviours and strategies. So, what to do if you're feeling sad, anxious, timid and angry? Of course, these emotions are all normal — we all feel sad, angry, anxious, worried, or down sometimes but when these emotions start interfering with our daily living, something needs to be done. Prevention is the best medicine so helping children and young people to learn calming techniques as well as whom to go to if they need help is important. Children and young people can keep adding to their suggestions as they learn more. Chapter 10 specifically addresses how to help children relax and reduce anxiety and tension.

Below is an example of Jamie and what he did with his class.

> In my class we have a big poster where each student has written what they do to feel better. They had some great suggestions such as pat their cat, play basketball, get a hug, sit with a friend. Every day I ask my students what they are doing today to feel good about themselves. They have to choose one thing and it helps them start the day off in a positive manner. — *Jamie, teacher for five years*

Media literacy is very important for school-age children and young people and so basic education in schools for all years should include guidance on how to interpret the media and sociocultural messages about body image. Children and young people should be encouraged to not just accept the messages they are exposed to but rather to look at them critically. Talking about realistic bodies is important so that children and young people have a broader view of what a normal body looks like at different ages. This sets them up to have more healthy relationships with their own bodies as well as their eating and exercising habits.

In schools, when it comes to *physical education,* aim classes at all fitness levels so as not to isolate those children and young people who may be overweight or less active and fit than others. You want to encourage everyone to participate. This can be hard as children going through puberty can be very self-conscious about their bodies. Be sensitive to this. Focus less on competition between peers, and instead emphasise success as taking part and trying one's best. As a parent or carer, encourage your child to get out and about, catch the bus to school, walk home, ride their bike and provide opportunities for physical activity. You doing the same sends a positive message. Of course, safety is paramount and schools and other parents can assist in monitoring our children so they are safe when at, and going to and from, school. As well, your local council can assist with providing safe streets and parks for children to play in.

Schools are good avenues for reaching parents and carers about what children and young people are doing and how they can help and encourage participation. As a parent or carer, encourage your child to participate in school activities and talk to them about why they don't want to engage. What is the issue and how can you help them solve it? Talking to teachers and counsellors can help when you have children who are very self-conscious or worried about their appearance.

If parents are concerned about the texts, Facebook posts or Instagram messages their child is receiving from peers, the school should be notified and action taken. Cyberbullying is harmful and should not be tolerated. Chapter 7 deals with this issue.

Chapter summary

- Trying to be a positive role model to children and young people is not easy especially when we have our own body hang-ups and negative experiences.

- Children look up to us for guidance in life and so it's our role, as adults, to provide them with the best education possible.

- We need to educate children about healthy physical and mental health, how to deal with teasing, how to have healthy interactions with others and how to love life and their experiences in it.

- If you're careful with your own self-talk, conversations with others and how you talk about weight, shape and size, this will help.

- Promote uniqueness and difference in individuals and how to respect and value yourself and others.

- If you need more professional support and guidance, seek the parent and carer mental health services in your area.

Boys to men — talking to boys about body image

> I have been a physical education teacher for a few years now and seen many boys shy away from playing sport, swimming, getting changed in the change room, or any other attention drawn to their bodies. It reminds me of when I was their age and I was teased for being 'fat'. It was the class joke, Brian the fatty. It was horrible and it messed with my confidence and sense of self. Part of the reason why I became a teacher was to help boys develop into confident men. I've always loved sport but when I was bullied I gave it up for a while. When I teach adolescent boys now, I tell the boys to focus on the function of their bodies and what their bodies can do rather than what they look like. I try to promote body acceptance and inclusion for all. I'm very quick to intervene when I see a boy being bullied particularly when it comes to his body, as I know myself how much of an impact it can have. Being a good role model is important and I talk to the boys about body image and how to support each other into being confident young men. — *Brian, physical education teacher*

This chapter covers male body image, what the unique concerns of males are, why they have these worries, and how to help, whether you're a teacher, counsellor, parent or carer.

What might surprise you about male body image is how common it is for males at all ages to worry about the appearance of their body, including its size, shape, muscle tone, as well as concern about specific features such as facial structure and thickness of hair. Just like women, they can become very self-conscious about their body or part of their body, particularly as they develop into adolescence and adulthood. Surveys of boys and young men, for example, have found that body image concerns are number one, ahead of concerns about school, relationships, family and career. The difference to girls and young women though, is that boys and young men typically suffer in silence, perceiving that talking about body worries will be seen as not 'masculine' or not 'tough' enough. So it's important that we're knowledgeable and sensitive to boys' body image and aware of warning signs of body image concerns and how to help.

Even minor concerns over appearance can lead boys to be self-conscious about their bodies, particularly when on display such as the beach, swimming, in the change room with other boys, and playing sport. This self-consciousness can then lead a boy to miss out on sport, being with friends, skip meals and feel anxious when exercising, particularly if overweight or perceived as 'too thin', and worry about what others may be thinking. You often see this at school where boys may not engage with others on the sporting field or seemingly shy away from making friends or even hanging out with girls because they're getting teased for their appearance. Boys are victims of teasing for their bodies just like girls and this can have a significant effect on their self-esteem. This teasing can come from both genders as well as from the adults in a child's life. Go to Chapter 7, which is on teasing and bullying, for specific help with this.

It's important not to minimise the issue for boys as they can really struggle as they go through puberty and trying to meander the media, particularly social media, and what is seen as 'acceptable' in terms of their looks and behaviour. Dieting in boys, for example, is quite common, as is obsession with muscle building activities. Often boys are laughed at for having body image and mental health issues and this reduces their help seeking. So make sure, as an adult, you are available and willing to talk to boys about this topic and take them seriously. Counsellors in particular are great assets to helping boys on a one on one basis with body dissatisfaction. Before you can help others though it's important to address your own body image issues.

Address your own body image issues

You don't have to have the most positive body image yourself to help boys but it helps if you can role model positive behaviours and help seeking. If you're a dad or male teacher, carer or helper, and you yourself have body image concerns, it's important to acknowledge these concerns, as they will influence your role modelling to boys and the way you talk to boys about body image. For example, you may be worried about your own body size and shape and need to be aware of how you manage and deal with this. Going through Chapter 2 on addressing your own body image issues should help, but you may also need professional help in order to feel better about your own body and self. While you're working on your own body image, be mindful of the language you use and how you talk about others' bodies including both male and female bodies.

What do boys and men worry about?

Boys tend to worry about not looking masculine enough before they hit puberty, as they're often smaller in size and lacking muscles. They may have a high-pitched voice and look more feminine. As a boy moves towards puberty he may worry that he is not as masculine as his peers and that he is not as muscular as other boys. They may start excessively exercising as a result or become obsessed with going to the gym or lifting weights. This can be dangerous if a boy is not properly supervised and trained. Boys who are overweight may also feel self-conscious and worry about being teased if they haven't already. As a result, they can feel pressured to diet to lose weight and like females, males too can fad diet and starve themselves to try and lose body fat.

As compared to younger males, older males, on top of worrying about their weight and looking toned and lean, tend to worry about losing their hair and worry more and more about growing bellies, as well as general aging. Older men are much more likely than younger men to worry about losing their looks and decreases in their youthfulness and muscularity as their bodies move further and further away from what the media promotes as the 'ideal' male figure (usually youthful, lean, muscular, with a full head of hair). Boys and men can also worry about the look and size of their genitals, perceiving that they should look a certain way and as a consequence, shy away from changing in front of others, using public toilets and being in intimate relationships. Much of this misguided information comes from exposure to pornography or listening to other boys and men, and even girls and women, talking about this body part. This is obviously a sensitive issue that is best managed by a trusting adult. This concern about the body can lead boys to feel anxious, depressed (even suicidal) and self-conscious, and must be taken seriously.

While taking pride in your appearance is normal and healthy, when these thoughts become obsessive, they have the potential to cause considerable harm and a condition known as muscle dysmorphia can occur. *Muscle dysmorphia* is a condition where a male perceives his muscles and body size to be smaller than they actually are. Often these males are already quite muscular, but are on a relentless pursuit to define their bodies even further at the expense of their health and happiness. They seem obsessed by their body and withdrawn from other activities. You can notice this by the way a boy talks, often continuously about people's appearance, fitness and muscle building, and never being happy with their own appearance. They may suffer from depression, anxiety and suicidal thinking as well as becoming addicted to weight loss and body-changing products including drugs. Overcoming something like muscle dysmorphia usually requires professional assistance.

> As a youth worker I've worked with a lot of boys who are very concerned about their bodies. They are often embarrassed to tell anyone about their worries sometimes saying that it's a 'girlie' thing to worry about. It can take some of them several years even to come forward about their body dissatisfaction and by this stage it has often led to other mental health problems. I help boys put their body image in perspective and help them focus more on their achievements and successes. I highlight more positive role models and try to normalise body dissatisfaction in males. There's often quite a relief when they finally tell someone about their worries. — *Peter, youth worker*

Boys' body image and the media

Unlike girls and women, most boys aren't out to get thin, and in fact those boys who are seen as 'skinny' are often teased and made fun of and as a result, desire to increase their body size. They want to bulk up and get big muscles as they see this as a sign of masculinity. But this drive to achieve this look can be quite unhealthy in terms of both physical and mental health. Researchers have shown a significant relationship between boys' and men's exposure to muscular-ideal media and negative self-image and engagement in dangerous dieting and exercising behaviour. Social media, including online forums and blogs, make it easy for boys to seek and share information about diet and fitness and swap unhealthy ways of getting lean and bulking up in muscle quickly. Some boys go to extreme efforts to get a muscular, chiselled physique and much of this is learnt through their interactions on social media, usually with friends, and the Internet in general. So for parents and carers, it's important to be aware of what your child is watching, viewing and reading so you can educate them on what's 'real' vs what's not. Some parents choose to limit their child's access to Internet sites with parental controls. It is okay to monitor and limit your child's Internet use as this helps you understand what your child is exposed to and can open up conversations to address what's healthy and what's not. This is not specific to body image, as monitoring your child's media use is important for broader issues including Internet safety in general. Having conversations with the family about whom they talk to and about what, can also be insightful.

> In our house we all have dinner together most nights. This can be hard as we've all got different commitments throughout the week. But we try hard to be together as a family. We talk about our day and what we've been doing. We also talk about what we're thankful for each day and one positive thing that happened. Even on a bad day there is always something good that happened. My boys don't always open up about their worries at dinner, but I can tell when they're upset over something and I will try and talk to them later if I think something is up. My boys know they can always come to me and no topic is off limits. — *Elizabeth, mother of four boys aged 8,12,15,17*

Following are some activities and general guidelines for talking to boys about body image and health.

General guidelines for class activities

If you are a dad or male carer, teacher or counsellor, talking to boys separately to girls can be beneficial, as boys tend to have a different understanding than girls about the issue. It can also help to hear from a male who has experienced body image issues such as bullying, and how they overcame the issue. Boys will often have ideas about what they want to look like in the future and so it's important to help them understand body changes and explain what's real and what's media hype. Getting students to go through magazines and look at images of men and how they're portrayed in the media is a good way to engage students and get them thinking critically about the messages being sent out. Getting them to look at both how the 'ideal' male and female bodies are portrayed is important. Then challenging what is the reality.

Who are the people in a boy's life who they admire and why? You can bet it's got nothing to do with what they look like. They might admire sporting personalities because they're awesome players or certain male relatives because they're fun to be around or certain females because they're nurturing. You might like to talk about the men you admire and why, thinking about those who are positive role models.

School/parent activities

Media

As just discussed, the way men's bodies are portrayed in the media can make boys think that there is only one acceptable body type and shape. Given most boys bodies don't look anything like these images, this sets a boy up to be dissatisfied with his body in comparison. School teachers might choose to have a class exercise that centres on the media and how male bodies are portrayed and challenge boys' understandings around it. For example, talking to boys about how we used to see advertisements with men doing things with their bodies that were functional (like fixing or lifting things) but now we see men in the media objectified for their appearance. It is such images that make the male body one to be looked at and admired if it adheres to what is seen as 'ideal', and that bodies that deviate from the ideal (i.e., most bodies), are scrutinised. What we want our boys to do is to focus on the function of the body, what it can do, what it's capable of doing, despite what it looks like.

It's important to emphasise, just as with the 'idealised' images for women, that the physiques in the media are almost impossible for most men to achieve, particularly before puberty, and as men age. Boys can often think that these images are 'normal' and what a man 'should' look like. Talking to boys about the media images of 'idealised bodies' in magazines, video games, movies, music videos, and social media is important and including the reality vs fiction. Then contrasting this with images of people they admire for their talents, personalities, and qualities. Getting them to think of the men in their life that they admire and why, is a good way to get boys thinking beyond skin deep.

As a family you can avoid TV, movies, and magazines that promote stereotypes and outdated gender roles and get your children to question what they're viewing. How real is it? Help children see the reality of what they view for both females and males. You may like to go back to Chapter 1's activities in addressing 'idealised' media images.

Internet safety

Bodybuilding and fitness forums can promote risky training and unattainable body ideals that boys may pursue without checking with a doctor or coach, so make sure you're aware of what they're viewing. Also, boys can expose themselves to constant criticism by posting photos of themselves through social media. So educate them about the safety and pros and cons of doing this. Keep an eye on your boy's social media use, what they're viewing, who they're talking to and what about (without invading their privacy of course). Online, boys can feed their obsession in isolation so make sure you're open to discussing social media. As well, sometimes having the Internet positioned in a room where others can see them, rather than in their rooms, may be a strategy for keeping an eye on what your child is doing online. Talk to them about Internet safety. For example, you never know who you're actually talking to much of the time and whether that person may be a predator.

> As a coach I talk to my boys about the dangers of online forums focusing on body enhancement, as they're often quite unhealthy. I encourage my boys to talk to me if they're concerned about their body or thinking about starting a diet, taking supplements or changing their exercise. I want to promote fun and fitness, not body obsession. There's nothing better than seeing my boys have fun as a team and feel good about themselves. — *Ryan, year 10 soccer coach.*

Increase opportunities for communication

It's clear that negative self-image can affect boys' physical and mental health and we live in a culture that discourages boys from talking about their feelings making it much harder for parents, teachers and carers to detect a boy's body dissatisfaction and its impact. So it's important to ask and talk about feelings and body image in a comfortable way to help boys express how they're feeling. Some ways to do this include talking to boys one on one openly about the issue as well as teachers and counsellors talking to boys as a group about what body image is, how to take care of their bodies and the dangers of going to extreme measures to try to get their desired body. Your school could set up a lesson to talk to boys about the issues and encourage them to support each other and where to go to get help.

Talk about female body image and teasing

Discussing with boys the issue for girls is also important as often boys tease girls due to their looks. We need to educate our boys not to do this as it can be very damaging to a girl's self-esteem. It's often thought of as 'harmless' teasing but there really is no such thing as 'harmless' teasing. You will read in Chapter 7 on body bashing, about how to manage appearance teasing and some exercises to do at school. This is just as important for boys as it is for girls. Boys make fun of each other's appearance often in ways that are seen to be a 'joke' but are actually quite hurtful. Typical teasing for boys is around them being scrawny and not having hit puberty or for those that have, making fun of the changes in their voice or the hair on their face. Teach boys about being assertive and saying 'no' when they feel they need to, as well as trying not to take comments personally.

Accept compliments

Teaching boys to listen to those around them who love and care about them and give them compliments can really help particularly if this comes from another male.

Teach about healthy behaviours

Teaching boys to exercise for health, fitness and fun is important. This will make them feel more in touch with their bodies and healthier on the inside. Role model this yourself by being active. As well, encourage healthy eating through providing education about what a growing boy's body needs. You as a parent or carer need to provide healthy foods in the home. The canteen can also provide healthy snacks and meals. Helping boys understand about sleep, sleep hygiene, and getting enough hours (between 9–12 hours for a young person and as much as 14 hours for younger boys). As well, educating boys about the dangers of drugs and alcohol and safe sexual practices. Lastly, teaching boys about mental health and wellbeing in general is very important (see Chapter 9) so they can grow up strong and healthy in mind and body.

If you're worried about your child, talk to them about this. Listening to your child without judgement increases the chances they will come to you for help. If they need more help than you can offer, help your child to find someone suitable including a counsellor or psychologist.

Chapter summary

- Educate boys about body image issues specific to males.

- Normalise talking about body issues.

- Educate boys about the reality of the media vs the reality of real male bodies.

- Keep up with what your child is viewing on the Internet and be open to discussing it.

- Be available to boys if they want to talk and normalise talking about feelings and worries.

- Role model positive self-talk about your body.

- Don't tease others for their body size and shape.

- Focus on the function of the body rather than its appearance.

- Engage in healthy behaviours as a family or educator.

- Seek help if your boy seems preoccupied with his appearance or is engaging in risky behaviour.

CHAPTER 5

Media literacy — talking to children and young people about media messages and safe use

Everyone in our house used to be constantly switched on with our heads down and sending message after message, checking Facebook, uploading pictures of ourselves and our 'happy snaps' that we'd spent sometimes hours manipulating to 'look our best'. My partner would sometimes text or email me from the study whilst I was in the kitchen! We'd stopped 'talking' to each other. Actually sitting down to dinner and having a conversation was a rare event. We decided, as a family, that we'd lost the connection with each other and we wanted it back. So we came up with some family rules around when we would and would not be using our devices. We had a device curfew set where we'd switch off our devices at dinner time and then by 9 pm so everyone could get a good night's sleep. Of course we had some secret texting on occasion but it was important to all of us that we stay connected in the traditional sense of the word. We watched a movie the other night as a family and everyone said how enjoyable it was without our devices because we could really concentrate and get into the movie. — *Barry, father*

This chapter focuses on understanding the media, the messages it sends and how we respond. We'll start with an overview of what media literacy is and what the media is trying to communicate followed by ways to help children and young people live healthily in our digital world.

Children and young people today are growing up with easy and regular access to many different types of media and the media actively seeks to attract their attention and communicate messages (usually to sell products), which are often unhealthy or unhelpful. As such, it is important that we help children and young people understand the underlying messages and become wise to the ways that media producers try to influence our behaviour in both positive and negative ways. We call this 'media literacy' and it refers to the ability to understand the content of any medium — print, audio, video, or other, what it's trying to communicate, and how it's trying to influence you.

The media is pervasive in Westernised societies and we are constantly connected to it. It is nearly impossible for most people, especially youth, to go a full day without using or experiencing some type of media. The media is powerful and can influence our behaviour, feelings and thoughts, that's what it aims to do after all. So we, as adults, need to be aware of its influence, both positive and negative. Start by thinking about the week just gone. How often were you around the media and what did and didn't influence you and how and why? You were probably more influenced than you realise. Understanding your own media use and its influence on you can help you assist children and young people to be safe media users.

Obviously the media communicates messages about a wide range of things, but let's focus on the messages around body image, dieting, exercising, weight, appearance, and clothing. Have a think over the last week about the media you've been exposed to around body image and how it's made you feel about yourself and what it's influenced you to do.

What are the current media messages around body image?

The messages the media send are changing all the time. In fact, between me writing this book and you reading it there will have been several fads and trends taking place. It's important, as a parent, carer, and educator, to be aware of the messages children and youth are receiving. To do this involves you talking to your child about what they're viewing, reading, listening to, being sent by friends, including the sites your child is using or has come across, sometimes by accident. Then ask them what they understand from what they've viewed and correct misunderstanding or discuss potentially detrimental messages. For example, at the time of writing this book my young clients were talking about the 'thigh gap', having a waist the size of an A4 piece of paper, sexting (sending sexual messages to friends or people over the Internet), posting on Facebook pictures or messages of or about themselves, using Instagram (sending photos which can be edited) or Snapchat (sending instant messages and images that disappear after a few seconds). As well, some youth will spend hours digitally manipulating an image of themselves using computer technology such as Photoshop to be the 'best', 'most perfect' picture of them to send to others.

Talk to children and young people about these images as they will be receiving them from friends, relatives, and even strangers. Images can now be made sharper, lighter, colour corrected, cropped, cleaned, have objects added or taken away, skin blemishes taken away, body parts lengthened, shortened and the list goes on. It's not uncommon for youth to spend a lot of energy and time on 'perfecting' their image. It can become distressing to some, and compulsive and obsessive leading to very poor body image. Children and young people too can get competitive with each other trying to send the most 'perfect' picture they can, better than their friends'. So monitor their engagement with this sort of activity. Sometimes what seems harmless can be quite obsessive and anxiety provoking, so monitor how your child is feeling. Do they show signs of being anxious when they use social media? If so, you need to intervene.

It's also important that you know what websites children and young people are accessing. Some can be very detrimental such as pro-anorexia sites, dieting and weight loss sites, muscle building sites or sites about drug use to change the body. While not wanting to 'invade' your child's privacy, it is important that to some extent, you monitor what your child is viewing. Using parental controls on television and Internet is one way of 'controlling' some of this exposure. Often in schools there will be certain key words that will be used to block students' access to sites and you can set this up at home too through contacting your service provider.

Always be open with children about what you're doing and why but also be firm, you are the parent or carer and so are responsible for the children in your care — including their viewing behaviour and their mental health. Explain why you're doing what you're doing to increase understanding.

Rules around social media

Nowadays young people are constantly switched on. It is okay to have rules around social media and use. Often parents and carers struggle to put boundaries up around social media use, as it seems so normal to be always switched on. However, there are some negative consequences of constant social media use including obesity and ill health due to the lack of physical activity and exercise. Nothing beats face-to-face contact and encouraging children to get out and be active and interact with their friends in the flesh is important for their social skill development. Sleeping difficulties are common in children and young people who are always using social media as they can be on it at night, keeping them awake. Setting some rules around when devices will be switched off is important, as is role modelling this by parents and carers. If we are always switched on it sends a message to our children that this is normal and okay.

It is okay to have family rules around Internet safety and mobile phone safety to protect children and young people. Sometimes they will say this isn't fair and that all their friends have access so why can't they. But each family is different and you don't have to do what everyone else supposedly does. It's the same when it comes to drugs and alcohol. It's important that you do what you're comfortable with as the parent/carer/adult with a child, not what everyone else is doing. You can feel pressured to allow your child to do things you're not comfortable with. But children respond best when boundaries are set and the rules are clear. Knowing they can always come to you to talk about concerns and worries and that you are there to look out for their wellbeing is important. It's easier to work with children if you set boundaries from the start, otherwise it's harder to enforce as they grow. It is perfectly okay to say 'no' but explain why. Don't give in to pressure that 'all other parents are doing x so why aren't you'. Make sure you're clear with rules and boundaries and be consistent. If you're not, children will learn how and when they can bend the rules. At the same time be flexible, there are some occasions when a rule may not apply, for example, on school holidays bedtime might be later. Treat all your children the same but educate them that children at different ages have different rules. For example, bedtime, having friends over, the movies they can watch change as children age.

Always explain though why there is a rule as it helps children understand and accept it. Follow the rules yourself and lead by example. Use of mobile phones and devices is a classic where we often expect children to 'switch off' before bed but we don't do this ourselves. If a rule is set, you have to follow through. Talking to other parents can help, but remember, this is your family, and you have to be comfortable with your rules.

Class or Home Activity: Media literacy

Being media literate is important because it helps us understand how the media communicates and tries to influence us. It also helps us to be able to critically analyse the messages regarding body image and therefore make better choices over changes in attitudes, intended behaviour, or actual behaviour. You might like to do this as a class activity or parents and carers can do this at home. It's about getting children and young people to question what they're viewing and interacting with. Some questions to start a conversation might be to begin by looking at different media images such as TV advertising, magazines, and websites by choosing some popular ones children and young people have likely seen, and ask these questions to get them thinking critically:

- What is the message being sent and is it a healthy message?
- Why is this message being sent, what is the media's intention (i.e., to get people to buy products)?
- What lifestyles, values, and points of view are represented in this message and which ones are left out?
- What is a healthy and safe way to respond to this message (i.e., ignore it, talk about it, realise the opposite is true etc)?

This activity can be as long or short as you like. It will start children and young people critically analysing what they view rather than being subjected to it without understanding.

Class or Home Activity: Digital imaging

Here's an activity you can do with youth around digital image manipulation. Show some images of before and after digital manipulation (type in body image and digital imaging before and after in Google) and ask:

- What do they observe is different between the images?
- What has been changed about the image and why?
- Is this okay?
- Are we all trying to look the same and why?
- What's wrong with striving to look like these images?
- What about celebrating differences and diversity?
- What's great about being different?

Then, start a conversation around when is digital imaging too much? What is acceptable for you and why? Here you can talk about being more critical about media images. You want to get children and young people talking about what they're viewing and the reality. How far is too far?

In your school, you may allow some digital touch ups in school photos for example. It is common that some schools will allow blemishes and pimples to be removed or complexions cleared. But is this okay? Or not? Think about the message this sends to students. Is it a help or hindrance?

Class or Home Activity: Media messages

A great activity to get children and young people engaged in addressing the messages behind the media is to get them to flick through some magazines and ask the following questions:

- Choose an image of a male or female (it's best to use popular magazines your students/children would be reading).
- What message is the advertiser trying to make?
- What do you think about the image?

- How does it make you feel viewing the image? (here you're trying to demonstrate how images in magazines can affect our mood and thoughts about ourselves)
- What is the message trying to sell?
- Is this a healthy message to be selling and why and why not? (this gets children and young people to think critically about the media rather than just accepting it)

Finish with a discussion about what children and young people can do to feel good about themselves. As suggested in Chapter 1, finish all activities with a self-esteem boosting exercise. Get them to write lists about what helps their mind and bodies feel good.

Chapter summary

- We can't escape the media but we can respond to it in healthy ways and choose how it makes us feel about ourselves.

- Adults are important educators of children and young people around social media and digital images.

- Get children and young people being critical of media messages.

- Always highlight the positives of diversity in body and qualities.

- It's okay to set rules around media use at home.

- As an adult, role model the behaviour you want to see in children and young people. Lead by example.

CHAPTER 6

Puberty explained — help, my body is changing!

> What is happening to my body? It's as if someone has taken it over without my permission. It's growing in funny places and at different rates. My voice is different, I have hair on my body and I don't fit into my school uniform anymore. I can see other boys are changing too. My physical education teacher talked to us boys last week about puberty and what we can expect. He told us to embrace it and celebrate it as we're becoming men. I like the sound of that but it's really weird watching my body change. My uncle Pete has been talking to me too about his experiences when he was growing up. It helps to know its normal and that every boy goes through it. — *Andrew, age 13*

This chapter discusses the exciting for some, but confusing and embarrassing for others, topic of puberty for both boys and girls. It goes through what puberty is and the changes that occur and how to talk separately to boys and girls. It's best to prepare children well before puberty hits to make the transition as easy as possible.

As a teacher, it is your job, as well as parents and carers, to educate children and young people about puberty and the changes that occur. Starting to educate children before puberty hits is a good idea so children are prepared for this change. It's important to be open to questions as well as helping them seek out other resources for help. Depending on your school's policies and religious beliefs and teachings, will determine how you talk to children and young people about puberty and bodily changes. It's important that parents and carers are aware of the education children are provided in schools so they can follow up with questions and corrections to misunderstandings at home. Try to talk as comfortably as possible. Students will be embarrassed and uncomfortable especially those who might have hit puberty already. So it's important to be sensitive and ensure the class is prepared to be respectful to each other before the discussion begins. Having other teachers, the school nurse, counsellors and pastoral care teachers available to assist students with questions and concerns after this education is important. As well, leading them to appropriate educational materials to get more information. The youth centres in your area often have good resources.

For parents and carers of young children, early education is important so children are prepared for the changes that are going to occur. Starting to explain expected changes early will help your child more easily transition as their body develops and changes. You have to judge where your child is at in terms of education about puberty. Some children will develop much earlier than others so it's important they are prepared.

Some suggestions for ways to talk to children and young people about puberty

Puberty is a word used to describe the change that occurs as our bodies go from being a child to an adult. Everybody goes through it and you can't stop it. It doesn't matter where you live, whether you're a boy or girl, what race you are, or what beliefs you have, you will go through puberty. Puberty is universal and occurs to everybody in every country. Often these changes are quite rapid and we can worry and stress that our bodies are changing without our control. It's important for children to understand what puberty is and what changes to expect so they can be more relaxed about it. Make sure you are relaxed too when talking about puberty. Try not to get embarrassed and treat it like any other education.

The reason why our bodies go through puberty is because hormones are being released by the brain that affect different parts of our bodies. Growth spurts are normal and you can notice that all of a sudden your clothes aren't fitting in different places. Girls and boys can feel a bit awkward about these changes and so it's important to realise it is completely normal and to talk to others and ask for help to cope.

Talking to girls

You can say something along these lines. For girls, the hormones that are released by the brain as they go through puberty make a girl able to produce eggs that enable her to become pregnant if she's trying for a baby. You can emphasise here that even though girls won't want to have a baby until they're older, their body still gets prepared for this at an early age. They also prepare a girl's body for having a baby by growing breasts and hips to feed and carry a baby. Girls can worry about these changes perceiving them as getting 'fat' so it's important to emphasise these changes as normal. Another hormone that's produced by these eggs is called oestrogen and this makes a girl get her period. It's also responsible for making a girl's hair grow on her body and girls will see thin hair growing all over their body including under their arms as well as around their genital area called pubic hair. Boys grow pubic hair too. You sometimes need to reassure girls as they sometimes jump to the conclusion that when they hit puberty they will get pregnant. Talking about reproduction and safe sex can be covered in another education module.

For girls, getting their period can be distressing as they produce blood. It's important to emphasise that this is completely normal and happens to every woman. Encourage them to share and talk to their friends as they will be going through it too but not necessarily at the same time. Adult women can help guide girls as to what to do to manage their period. Reassure girls that their teachers will talk to them about what's happening to their body and why girls get their period. Tell them that if they're worried or they have questions, they can ask a trusted adult who can help.

As said before, it's quite normal for girls to be unhappy with puberty as they get curvier and often this is quite a shock. Breast development in particular can be embarrassing and sometimes girls can be very self-conscious and shy away from sport and other activities where the body is on show. Normalise this and encourage them to embrace puberty and their body because they can't change it and it means they're becoming a woman, and it's awesome to be a woman! You might like to tell them that getting breasts means they can wear nice bras and your body changing is a great excuse for new clothes!

Talking to boys

For boys, the hormone that's released is called testosterone and this hormone is responsible for growth in height, bones, muscles, genitals, hair, as well as making a boy able to produce sperm so he can be a father and produce a baby (when he's ready). So tell boys that they'll notice other boys growing taller and broader, as well as deepening of their voice. Boys also start to grow more hair on their bodies including their face, underarms and around their genitals. It's very hard to cover up this growth on the face as it's very obvious. It's important to realise that every boy goes through puberty at a different pace so each boy will look different. This is completely normal and everyone goes through these changes. It can be helpful for boys to talk to the men in their lives so they understand what's happening and are reassured it's normal. Going shopping with boys to buy raisers and nice smelling deodorant and shaving cream can make boys feel more enthusiastic about this change.

Teasing can occur between boys as they go through puberty and change at different rates. It's important to highlight the importance of not teasing and rather supporting each other through changes. Boys can become embarrassed, for example, if they're the first to grow hair or their voice to change, and vice versa if they're one of the last to go through it.

As opposed to girls, boys often like puberty because their shoulders grow broader and muscles start to develop. They will also find working out with weights and doing muscle building sports more effective during and after puberty to change the body. For some boys, they get a bit of hair growth on the chest which can be distressing. Again, talking to men can help normalise this and reduce distress. Watch out for boys you can see are self-conscious and help normalise their experience. Some boys will want to hide their bodies or be embarrassed as they start to notice changes. Again, providing adults that they can talk to for help is great. This might be a coach, a relative, a family friend, or an older brother for example.

For both genders

The start of puberty for most starts roughly between ages 8 and 13 years but for some it can start earlier or later. Tell children that they may notice that some of their peers look older than others because they have gone through puberty earlier and quicker. Everybody develops at a different rate and we can't really control this. So we must celebrate it and not tease one another for the changes that occur. This can sometimes be when body image and eating disorders start, as the body changes in a way that a child or young person doesn't like.

One of the things that can be upsetting for both genders is getting acne (pimples). This is caused by the hormones in the body. Reassure children and young people that it's normal to get pimples on your face and sometimes on other parts of your body. If they're worried or self-conscious they can talk to someone they trust. Doctors and dermatologists can help medically with acne if it's very distressing.

Talk also about body odour. Unfortunately as we go through puberty we also start to sweat under our arms and this can produce a smell. Sweat glands are also more active all over the body so children and young people may experience sweating in other areas of their body even when they're not active. There are lots of ways to help control this including showering, wearing deodorant, changing clothes more regularly, among other ways. Encourage children to talk to parents or carers who can help manage this. Going out and experimenting with new things to make the body smell nice can be fun for boys and girls.

Another area that changes is the genitals. Both genders can get quite distressed by this, not understanding the changes that occur. Erections for boys in particular can be embarrassing. Talking to teachers, carers and parents is encouraged to find out how to manage these changes. Remind children and young people again that it can feel as if their body is out of control with all these changes, so ask questions, read about it, and seek support. Remember that this change is totally normal and happens to everyone. State that eventually everyone evens out and everyone becomes an adult and these changes stop. Encouraging children and young people to embrace puberty as an exciting time of their life and an important stage that everyone goes through, going from a child to an adult.

You may even like to share stories of your own journey through puberty and how you handled changes.

Some guidelines for adults talking about puberty

When talking about puberty it's often best to split children or young people into gender groups so you can have a more targeted discussion. As well, it will encourage more question asking and reduce some embarrassment. At the same time, both genders need to know what happens to the opposite sex too. You might like to start by asking your group what they know about puberty in them and the opposite sex and then you're able to correct misunderstandings. Talk about the points in this chapter and any other education that your school usually includes. Each school will be different in terms of what is discussed, particularly schools with certain religious overtones.

If you're a parent or carer, talk to your child openly and be available for the many questions they might ask. If you don't know the answer, be open to helping them find out. They may not feel comfortable with asking you all questions so having someone else like a family friend or relative who is also there to assist is a good idea. It's important that you be as comfortable as possible when talking to your child and you target your education at an age appropriate level. Talking about puberty before it happens is crucial as well as normalising the changes and reassuring your child that everyone goes through this process. Start by asking your child what they know and understand about puberty and then correct misunderstandings. You might even like to practise with another adult before you talk to your child.

Chapter summary

- Puberty can be an exciting time for a young person but also have its challenges in terms of body image.

- Talking to children before they hit puberty about what to expect can make the transition smoother.

- Be available to children and young people to answer their questions.

- Normalise puberty.

- Encourage your child to focus on the positives of becoming an adult.

- Provide your child with different sources of correct information such as youth health websites, pamphlets and other resources.

- Emphasise the importance of respecting others and not teasing peers going through changes.

CHAPTER 7

Teasing and body bashing — it's not okay!

I remember very clearly being teased at school. It started at around year 4 when I was 9 years old. I was a little chubbier than the others kids and they used to call me names, usually when no adult was there to witness it. At first I thought they were just joking around but then it became a regular name calling — 'hey fatso, pass me the ball' and the like. I became really self-conscious and at one point actually stopped eating because I thought if I lost weight the teasing would stop. I did lose weight but then was teased for being 'scrawny'. I just couldn't get it right. Those harsh words stuck with me for a long time and affected my body image as an adult. I'm now in my 30s and teach sport studies in high school. I don't tolerate body bashing or body teasing of any kind. My students know exactly where I stand on this issue. Everyone is to be respected in my class. — *Edward, teacher*

This chapter covers the important issue of bullying and how it affects children, young people and adults. It highlights the difference between 'teasing' and 'bullying' with suggestions as to how to prevent and stop bullying.

Cyberbullying in particular is discussed here with strategies to protect children and young people.

We know that teasing occurs and that bullying is a problem in the school and work environment whether this be about appearance or not. It happens to people of all ages, races, genders and religious backgrounds. We know that bullying can result in mental health problems, including depression (even suicide ideation), anxiety, and stress, and where there is appearance teasing, body dissatisfaction and body image issues, even disordered eating. Typical appearance teasing centres on a person's weight, shape, height, hair, clothing and facial characteristics. Also, peers who engage in 'fat talk' can make body dissatisfaction worse and eating issues may develop too. Let's talk here about what teasing and bullying are and how to work with children and young people around these issues.

Most children will experience teasing at some point in their life and you will likely recall teasing when you were young too. Children often tease each other because they're trying to be funny and get a reaction from another child. Teasing can be positive when it demonstrates closeness and affection for another person. For example, as an adult, you may have friends that playfully tease you in ways they think are funny and you may go along with it and tease them back. Sometimes teasing can be used to reduce conflict and tension too. Teasing is okay when the receiver knows the person is joking and they don't take offence or are hurt by the teasing. For example, playful teasing about always being late with your friends, or your sport team losing, or trying to make light of a situation by making a joke might be okay in your friendship circle. However, teasing can be hurtful and harmful and unfortunately most people have experiences of this type of teasing in their life. This sort of teasing can been seen as critical, embarrassing, and alienating, really hurting the receiver. Teasing about physical appearance, for example, is usually hurtful.

You will remember teasing from your own upbringing where people might have commented on the colour of your hair, your skin, your body shape and size, what you're wearing, and it can have a lasting effect where you feel self-conscious throughout your upbringing and even into adulthood. So make your home a positive one by speaking well of each other and what makes each member worthwhile.

Teasing vs bullying

A question of importance is the difference between *teasing* and *bullying*. *Bullying* is when a person is distressed by the teasing and it is hostile and deliberately hurtful. Also, where there is a power imbalance such as teasing of a younger child by an older child, the teasing is repetitive, the person being teased is hurt emotionally, and the teasing causes distress. It can occur over a person's appearance or for something else. You've probably heard about or witnessed bullying in the workplace where someone is repeatedly targeted and harassed and they may go on stress leave as a result. Bullying is never okay in any shape or form. It can cause a person to develop depression, anxiety, become suicidal and if body related, contribute to the development of an eating disorder. The person being bullied may not always show how distressed they are by the bullying, often putting on a brave face. Many people suffer in silence. It's quite common, for example, for boys to put on a strong face and grin and bear it.

So what should you do if you know a child or young person is being bullied?

You must intervene. If you're a teacher or counsellor, talking to the bully about their unacceptable behaviour is important and stating that it won't be tolerated. For parents and carers, it's important to report it to the school so they can intervene.

When talking to the bully (or if it's bullies)

Talk to them each individually, ask why they are teasing the child or young person and talk about why this isn't okay. Talk about how the bully can find better ways to communicate and engage with other children. Some children and young people tease because they see others doing it including their peers or parents/carers. You must talk about why that's not okay. Perhaps they do not have the skills to make friends or behave in gentler ways. If so, talk to them about how to interact appropriately with others. Ask the child to take the perspective of the child they are teasing. How would you feel if someone did that to you? You may need to speak with the child's parents or carers about their behaviour and how the parents or carers are going to manage this behaviour at home. This can be tricky especially if you're working with a non-responsive or defensive parent or carer. Falling back on school rules is a good way of making it clear what the consequences will be for this child.

For the child that is being bullied

It's important to talk to them too. Ask them if they're okay and let them know that you are going to help them and that bullying is not okay. Discuss how the child or young person can be assertive and what they can do to protect themselves. Let them know that you can be trusted and you will help put an end to bullying.

Class Activity: Talking about bullying

This is best done at the start of the school year before teasing has a chance to start. It's very important that you make the class clear that bullying is not tolerated in your school and that even 'playful' teasing can hurt. Talk about treating each other respectfully and how your school prides itself on each individual being treated fairly and equally. Ask the class what respecting each other looks like and how they know they're being respectful. Inform students of what to do if they see someone being teased. For example, don't stay silent, speak up, and talk to an adult if needed. Students may acknowledge that they have teased or bullied someone in the past and talk about how they can repair that relationship; for example, apologising, and being kind and respectful. Inform students that they don't have to feel bad about what they may have done before that wasn't very nice if they make amends and acknowledge, apologise, and make an effort not to say mean things to that person again. Come up with some class rules so everyone knows how they should be treated.

Positive role modelling

Children and young people are great observers of people's behaviour and you as an adult are being watched for how you relate to others, what you say, how you say it and the impact it might have on others. Obviously, you need to make sure that you are not bullying others and being careful that your 'playful' teasing is indeed communicated and received that way. You may have been bullied yourself growing up or even in the workplace now. Think about this and how it affects your approach to the children in your care. If you feel that your own experiences are negatively affecting you, seek help.

Social media and teasing

With the advent of social media, bullying is on the rise. We often call this cyberbullying where a person is bullied over social media. This can occur in children and adults and in many different forms. It's very important that schools, work-places and homes have strict policies and procedures for cyberbullying and bullying in person, to protect people. Where a school supports its students and makes families clear on the rules, there are better outcomes for students. You play a crucial role in stopping workplace and school based bullying. It is important for parents and carers especially to know how to block people from your child's social media so that you can protect them from exposure to the bullies. Get help from your service provider if needed. Encourage your child or young person to talk to you about what has happened and come up with a solution together. Children and young people can often be embarrassed to show an adult what they've been bullied for so have open communication, never laugh or brush it off as trivial, give your child attention and show you care and can help. This also goes for if your child talks about witnessing their peer being bullied. Standing up for others is important too.

Our peers can be a very positive influence on our body image and self-esteem. For example, when we're appreciated for who we are by our friends and we are not judged or made fun of, we feel good about ourselves and we can trust our friends. So encourage this in your class and home.

Being teased about weight

Although anyone can be bullied, teens who are underweight, overweight, or obese are at a higher risk of being bullied. They often are targeted because of the way they look. When a person is targeted because of their weight, this is called *weight teasing.* And research shows that when people are bullied because of their weight, they become dissatisfied with their bodies and this can lead to body image and mental health problems. How a person thinks about their body and themselves is heavily influenced by their peer's behaviour and how they internalise this. Some young people self-harm as a way to reduce distress over bullying so it's quite serious. There have also been incidences of young people suiciding due to bullying.

We are all taught about the importance of being a healthy weight. But for overweight children, losing weight is not easy and for those who are underweight, gaining weight may be hard. When on top of this battle to be a healthy weight you're being teased about your weight, a child can feel alone and helpless to change their situation. So make sure the child knows they have help and support from you.

So who are the people engaging in weight teasing? It's often thought that it's just mean people who are the bullies but it can also be the person's friends, teachers, coaches and even relatives, parents and carers. Sometimes people can think it's okay to make comments and that they're harmless or even helpful. Making negative comments to someone else about their appearance is never okay. If you're concerned about a child's health, there are more constructive ways of assisting without making negative comments. For example, you could take the approach that the whole family are going to spend more time having fun with activity and eating healthier so it's not the one person's problem. Talk to your GP, a nutritionist, school nurse, for assistance if your child needs to lose or gain weight for their health. Simple things such as making your family more active, having healthy foods in the house, reducing screen time and encouraging time out for stress relief can assist.

Role modelling negative impressions of people's weight

Adults can make supposedly 'harmless' comments about other people's weight and size in front of children and young people, modelling what is clearly unhealthy and unhelpful behaviour as acceptable. Comments can also be made about what someone is eating, making it a judgement about them. For example, 'look at that fat person eating that burger, no wonder they're fat'. This sends a clear message that the person making the comment thinks badly of the person they are commenting on. So children and young people learn from those around them what is and isn't acceptable. Make your family home and workplace a 'weight comment free zone' where judgement is not passed on what people look like.

People can also comment on what people are wearing, the exercise they do, the social activities they engage in, the people they hang out with, supposedly making 'helpful hints'. But in reality the words are judgmental and critical. When directly targeted, this can make people feel bad about themselves and their bodies. If you're concerned about what a child is wearing for whatever reason you need to be clear on whether your comment will be helpful or perceived as criticism. Of course, there will be times when you think what someone is wearing is inappropriate, for example, a young person wearing something quite revealing. In these cases it might be helpful to assist the young person to make a safer choice. However, do not criticise the child or young person.

How to work with children where their weight is a health risk

We all want our children to be healthy, and being overweight or underweight can be unhealthy and not good for their well-being. Children are often teased about this too. So finding a way to manage it without making their weight an issue can be tricky. Sometimes as a result of teasing for example, young people can overeat as a way to 'cope'. This of course furthers the problem with their weight and the way they feel about themselves. There also is some evidence that overweight children who are subjected to weight-related teasing are less likely to exercise because they feel self-conscious and feel that they are more likely to be made fun of. This discourages healthy behaviours and exercise that compounds the problem. So talk about it as a family or class — we're going to work on being healthier and drinking water, eating nutritious foods and exercising for fun.

Making sure that there are physical activities at school that all students can participate in for any fitness level. At home, you can focus on boosting your child's self-esteem and building resilience by focusing on positive attributes and qualities and not on weight. Also avoid congratulating your child on weight loss. Instead, encourage them to participate in activities that will build self-confidence and congratulate success in those areas. Doing so will show your child that their worth is not tied up in their appearance. You might like to assist children in coming up with some clever come backs if they're being bullied to help them stick up for themselves, helping them to be assertive.

Class Activity (and also helpful to parents and carers): Talking about body bashing

Talk to the class about what they understand *body bashing* to be. Highlight that it can be to others or to yourself when you're in a group. For example, it's not uncommon for teenage girls to sit around talking about the parts of their bodies they don't like and sharing their body dislike or even hatred. This is not healthy as it encourages put-downs and reduces self-esteem even though girls may think it's about 'fitting in' with their peers. It may be helpful here to split the class into genders as girls typically talk about fat (often called *fat chat*) and boys tease each other in terms of puberty and perceived 'manliness'. Ask the group about whether they feel that this kind of talk is seen as a way to bond with their peers and what would be alternative ways to bond that are more positive? Ask them — wouldn't they rather bond over something positive then something negative? Also, asking them to think about what it would feel like if your friends gave each other compliments and talked well about their bodies such as focusing on the function of the body and what it can do? Such compliments might be about sporting talents, being a leader, standing up for others, being a good friend, and so on. Ask them — would we feel better? Then get them to come up with a list of things to say and do with friends that boost each other up rather than put each other down.

For managing 'fat talk' or 'body bashing' it's important to state that there's nothing wrong with being proud of your body and yourself. That you should spread this around as well as celebrating achievements.

Here are some things you can talk to the class about to stop body bashing. Ask them to think about how they do this and add their own examples.

- Encourage students to go beyond appearance. Don't look at someone and think about their flaws or what's wrong with their body, look beyond this and see the person for who they are. What do you like about this person? If the students know each other well, you can do an exercise where each student writes something positive about each other student in the class.

- If you hear others teasing someone or putting someone down, don't join in and don't be silent. We need to stand up for each other and point out to the bully that their behaviour is not okay. It's not okay to criticise or insult people.

- Be assertive. If someone body bashes you or a friend, tell them that their comments offend you and you want them to stop. And stick up for your friends who do this too.

- Let go of the jealously you may feel towards others. Rather, appreciate individuals in your life for their differences to us. It's okay to admire people but we don't have to feel down on our-selves in comparison. Everyone has their unique strengths, including you.

- Share what you like about someone. Giving each other comple-ments and verbalising that you think someone has a nice personality, is funny, is thoughtful, creative, and so on.

- Accept compliments and thank the person giving it. People respond well when we thank them for the complement rather than dismissing it.

- Let go of the way the media tell you that you should look like or what others should look like. Be your own person.

- Make being happy and healthy in your own skin an ongoing goal.

- Everybody is beautiful and so look for what is beautiful in every person you come across.

Guidelines for school policies around bullying

What are the school policies around bullying? Make sure you know them. This is important to remind your students that body bashing is not okay in your school and what the consequences are. In fact, teasing of any sort is not okay and students need to be reminded about this. Talking about the school values should help, such as reminding students that they are expected to respect each other and treat each other with dignity.

It's not uncommon for schools to experience body bashing and teasing over social media and there have been many an incident where a student has been spoken negatively about over Facebook for example. This needs to be stopped as it is very detrimental to young people's mental health.

Educating parents and carers about the school's policies on teasing is important as well as tips on how to monitor social media use. Parents and carers need to be made aware of what their child is posting and reading on social media and be able to take action if their child is bullying another or posting inappropriate material.

Chapter summary

- There's a difference between teasing and bullying.
- Bullying is never okay and can affect a person's mental health.
- Body bashing leads to negative body image.
- Be mindful of your own attitudes towards people of different appearances and what you say about them.

- Talk about the policies and procedures for reporting and dealing with bullying.

- Assist children to be more assertive if they're being bullied.

- Talk to your class about speaking respectfully about others.

- Go beyond appearance and look for what a person has to offer as an individual.

- Get help for yourself if you're dealing with a child or young person who is very distressed by bullying.

CHAPTER 8

Diet free zone — the dangers of eating disorders and how to help

> I noticed my daughter was getting thinner and thinner and at first thought she was just being 'healthy' and taking care of herself. But it got to the point where she would become extremely anxious and upset if she couldn't exercise or if I cooked her dinner in a way she didn't like such as putting 'too much' oil in it. She ended up developing anorexia nervosa and it was frightening. We sought help as a family because we knew that as parents, we had to intervene. She got better with help and gradually restored her weight to a healthy range. It took a lot of work though, and we all had to work together as a family. I wish I'd picked up on the warning signs earlier but I never imagined my bright, active, social daughter would ever be susceptible to this. — *Helen, mother of two*

In this chapter we'll talk about eating disorders, psychological conditions that centre on extreme concerns about the size and shape of the body. As well, eating disorders involve engagement in dangerous behaviours for the body and mind as a person attempts to try and make their body look like they desire or what they think is 'acceptable' in terms of appearance. We will talk about what disordered eating looks like, how common it is, tips on what to look out for and how to prevent and intervene.

Disordered eating: What is it?

Disordered eating refers to a wide range of unhealthy eating behaviours that occur as a result of body image dissatisfaction. Often the person is highly distressed with regards to their perception of their appearance and seeks to control their eating. It occurs in both males and females. Eating disorders are at the extreme end of disordered eating. Disordered eating has a very negative impact on a young person's emotional, social and physical wellbeing. So it should be taken seriously and acted on quickly.

Some obvious signs of disordered eating are, constant comments about weight, shape and size of self and others, comments about food, difficulty sleeping, fatigue, looking malnourished (or in contrast, putting on a lot of weight) or having difficulty concentrating. As well, eating is often either very controlled or completely uncontrolled (in the case of binge eating). Disordered eating often affects young people's social life as they can't eat with others or find it extremely anxiety provoking. You may even notice lunches coming home uneaten and a child saying that they're not hungry most of the time. Emotional warning signs are anxiety and depression in children. Typically, disordered eating tends to occur in high school aged children rather than primary school aged, but fussy eating can certainly occur in young children and there are cases of primary school aged children with eating disorders.

Some of the signs of disordered eating that you see in both children and adults are:

- Skipping meals and stating that they're not hungry; or in contrast, constant eating.

- Not eating in social situations or trying to control the situation where food is involved.

- Binge eating (eating large quantities of food in a discrete period of time) and seeming to be out of control in their eating. It's not just overeating on occasions.

- Dieting.

- Obsessive calorie counting and measuring of foods.

- Constant weighing of the body.

- Talking about foods being 'good' and 'bad' and anxiety when 'bad' foods are eaten.

- Self-induced vomiting or signs of this such as a puffy face, blood shot eyes, dehydration.

- Self-worth based on body shape and weight (i.e., your child may refuse to leave the house until they are looking 'perfect').

- Constant comments about food, body shapes of self and others.

- Misusing laxatives or diuretics or using diet pills for perceived weight loss or avoidance of weight gain.

- Being very picky over eating and needing food to be prepared in a certain way.

If you notice any of these signs in your child, get help immediately. There are very effective treatments available by psychologists to help young people with body image and eating issues.

Let's look at Sophie. Sophie is a healthy young girl in year 10, aged 15, but she's been worried about being 'too fat' since year 7. She has tried lots of diets sometimes starving herself.

I felt really unhappy with my body and I thought that if I just lost some weight I'd feel better. So I tried dieting, lots of dieting, different combinations of eating this and not that. My weight went up and down and I didn't feel any better. Then I realised that the way to feel better about my body was to stop torturing it. My body hasn't done anything wrong, it doesn't need to be punished through losing weight. I just have to accept it, care about it and treat it well. When I eat well and have fun with my friends I don't worry about my weight. I know my body is changing too and talking to my friends often helps as they are going through change also.

It can sometimes be hard to talk to young people about body image, food, and weight and they will often prefer to talk to their friends rather than teachers, counsellors or parents. However, being available to children and young people is important. Letting them know that you are there if they want to talk. You can be a better source of accurate information compared to your child's friends for example.

Class Activity: Talking about dieting

For teachers, you may want to talk to girls and boys on their own about eating disordered behaviour and what to do. This results usually in a more open discussion and each gender is likely to be more comfortable asking questions about body image with their same gender peers. Here are a few examples of what to talk to the class about. Educating young people, particularly girls, about how important it is to not swap stories with their peers about dieting because this can trigger unhealthy behaviours in someone else. State that if they're worried about their weight, size or eating, then its best to discuss this with an adult who can help. Let students know who in the school they can go to for help.

Here's an activity on 'normal' eating. Ask the students to talk about what is normal and not normal and correct misunderstanding. Young people are often confused as to what 'normal' eating is so go through the following.

It is **normal** to:

- Sometimes be conscious about your appearance especially at important events (but this should never be anxiety over appearance or stop a child or young person doing day to day activities).

- Eat more on some days and less on others depending on your activity level or the weather for example.

- Eat some foods just because they taste good and not feel guilty about this.

- Have a positive attitude towards food as opposed to finding food and eating anxiety provoking.

- Not label foods with judgement words such as 'good', 'bad', 'clean'.

- Overeat occasionally (such as at special events such as birthdays and Christmas).

- Undereat occasionally (such as when you're not well).

- Crave certain foods at times.(You might talk to both genders about the effects of hormones on appetite for example).

- Treat food and eating as one small part of a balanced life as opposed to being consumed by thoughts about food and eating.

- Prefer certain clothes compared to others because of the way they look on your body. It's normal for example, that young people spend a lot more time getting ready than at other ages but it shouldn't be causing distress (severe anxiety).

- Not be constantly dieting.

The dangers of dieting — teacher/counselor discussion guidelines

It is really important not to have students swapping stories about dieting. This is harmful. Talk about the dangers of dieting and why diets don't work. Following are some key points to talk through with young people so they understand the dangers of dieting and extreme weight loss methods. You might even get them to research the dangers of dieting themselves and contribute to the discussion from what they've learnt. Be mindful of not talking about 'diets that work' or about your own experiences in a negative way. Always point out that its normal to be a bit self-conscious about your body, but dieting isn't the solution to feeling better and there is lots of help available. Go through the following points if students have not already come up with them.

- Dieting is the greatest risk factor for the development of an eating disorder (there is a huge amount of research supporting this). This is because dieting labels foods 'good' and 'bad' and restriction is common for diets, which sets a person up to feel anxious if they eat something on the 'bad' list or they break a food rule.

- Boys diet too. Many boys in adolescence can start engaging in dieting behaviours to try and get more muscular or lose body fat. They often become fixated on eating certain foods, at the exclusion of others, making their diet unbalanced. So it's important that we look after our boys too and warning signs of a need to be concerned (see indicators of disordered eating).

- Dieting makes you hungrier as they are often restrictive and leave you feeling constantly hungry. Dieters can often ignore this hunger for a short time but such deprivation usually leads to food cravings that can be out of control and bingeing starts. This starve–binge cycle results in feelings of guilt, anxiety, and failure which make a person feel depressed and down on themselves. This cycle can continue throughout a person's lifetime and is a major risk factor in the development of an eating disorder.

- Diets disconnect people from their natural bodily responses. So instead of listening to hunger and satiety cues, dieters follow rigid rules around what and when they can eat. This is not a normal way to feed the body.

- Rising obesity rates coincide with the growth of the weight-loss industry and its profits. People spend a large amount of money on 'fad' diets and this often results in more eating of high calorie foods and weight gain in the longer term.

- Diets often leave a person constantly hungry and in some cases, lacking the necessary nutrients they need to maintain physical health and energy levels (draw students' attention to the fatigued feeling they get when they haven't eaten in a while).

- Dieting can reduce the body's metabolism (the rate it burns energy) and can make young people feel tired and have difficulty concentrating. Your body can get confused and therefore start to hold on to the nutrients it does receive leading sometimes to weight gain.

- Bad breath, fatigue, overeating, headaches, muscle cramps, constipation, sleep disturbance and loss of bone density (due to lack of calcium) are just some of the effects dieting can have on our bodies. Children and young people's growth can be stunted through dieting if they're not getting enough nutrients.

- Our bodies depend on food to function. Our heart, lungs, and brain can't function without food. We even need fuel to breathe and our brains need fat to think clearly and to reduce anxiety.

- Dieting and being unable to eat a variety of foods means you can't go out with friends and have fun as you're worried about the food that will be available.

- Having fun with food is part of life and dieting often stops us being able to do this.

It's important to reassure students that if they are dieting, they can stop, and an adult can help them put their eating back on a healthy track. The school nurse, dieticians, nutritionists and doctors can help.

The obsession with 'healthy eating': Orthorexia

> I just wanted to be healthier and so I started cutting out foods that were processed, then anything that wasn't 'natural' until I was hardly eating anything at all. I couldn't go out with friends as I couldn't guarantee that I would be able to eat something at the places they chose. I wouldn't eat what mum and dad cooked and I soon became malnourished. It was a slippery slope into an eating disorder. — *Melanie age 17*

Let's talk here about a type of diet that is becoming popular and so is important to talk to young people about. Orthorexia is an obsessive way of eating where a person will only eat what they perceive as 'clean' or 'pure' foods. What is usually meant by 'clean' foods are unprocessed foods and avoiding foods that contain sugar, salt and fat. It might also involve not eating meat, dairy and grains. Whilst this might sound like healthy eating it usually isn't as the person becomes obsessed with only eating certain foods at the exclusion of variety and balanced nutrition. For example, you might see children all of a sudden becoming vegetarian, vegan or 'clean' eaters for reasons of purifying the body, 'being healthy', 'looking after themselves', wanting to lose a 'little' bit of weight. Unfortunately, this way of eating usually is weight related and can quickly become out of control where a child becomes very distressed if they can't eat what they believe is 'good' food. They may become very picky eaters and will avoid eating with others and sharing food with others.

As with the eating disorders, the reasons for this type of eating is usually weight, shape and size focused. A child or young person will become anxious if they can't access the food they deem is 'clean' and distressed or guilty if they are made to eat a variation of their restricted diet. Mood swings are common and the child or young person may show signs of being malnourished. A growing child needs a variety of foods and nutrients so any restriction can have a very negative consequence on their physical and mental health.

For assistance it is best to consult a nutritionist, dietician, psychologist, doctor or counsellor. Anyone who has had an eating disorder should be strongly discouraged from this style of eating. Remember, as a role model, you need to be encouraging variety and so if you are following this sort of diet, you need to seriously consider its effects.

Eating disorders — introduction

Eating disorders are very serious mental health conditions that also affect physical health. These disorders have the highest mortality rates of any psychiatric illness. They completely take over a person's wellbeing and help should be sort immediately when warning signs are noticed. If you yourself are suffering from an eating disorder please seek help.

First, let's address the myths of eating disorders. If you ask the average person about eating disorders they will usually say they happen to young girls and it's where they lose a lot of weight. This is only partly true. Eating disorders do not discriminate by gender or age. There are incidences of children in primary school with eating disorders as well as the aged. One out of ten sufferers are males too. Some sufferers will under eat and some will overeat or a combination of the two. So what a person looks like is not a good sign of an eating disorder. For example, people with binge eating disorder will usually be overweight or obese.

For parents and carers, as soon as you notice a child in your care has a concern with their weight and size that is interfering with their happiness and the things they do, seek help. First point of call is your GP for a referral to a psychologist, specialised eating disorder clinics and other mental health specialists if needed.

Let's now talk about the different disorders. The *Diagnostic and Statistical Manual of Mental Disorders, Fifth Edition* (DSM-5) is used to diagnose eating disorders. Diagnosis helps professionals to identify the condition so they know what the appropriate treatment is to take. As well, it helps health professionals communicate with each other in a language they all understand. Diagnosis can often help sufferers put a name to their experience and therefore better understand themselves and their symptoms. When we understand what's happening to us, we're better able to make change.

Anorexia nervosa

This is the condition most people have heard about where a person severely restricts their intake of nutrients and loses a large amount of weight, often being malnourished. It's important to note though that some people with anorexia can seemingly be a 'healthy' weight. As with all the eating disorders, it's marked with a preoccupation with weight, size and shape and can occur in both genders. Here's an example of Paul.

> I was 25 when I first started dieting to lose weight. I'd put up with being called 'fat' for years and dabbled in drugs to try and lose weight and gain muscle in my teens. When I started dieting I lost a lot of weight and I liked my body. But it just kept going, I couldn't be 'thin' enough. People kept telling me I looked ill and this just spurred me on. I was diagnosed with anorexia nervosa, which I thought was stupid, I was a male and just looking after my health wasn't I? I eventually got help in my 40s. What a waste, 15 years of dieting and hating my body. With

treatment, I learnt to treat my body well and be comfortable in my own skin. Treatment was hard and long as I
was working on years of torment. I wish I'd got help
earlier or that someone had noticed I needed help. —
Paul, 45.

Some of the signs of anorexia to look out for:

- An obsession with weight, shape, size of self and others.

- Losing weight and possibly wearing layers to cover up
  weight loss (i.e., wearing jumpers in summer).

- Loss of periods in girls and low bone density due to the
  lack of calcium in boys too.

- Fatigue and lethargy due to lack of nutrients.

- Skipping meals or stating they're not hungry frequently.

- Avoiding eating with others.

- Seeming down a lot of the time and anxious especially
  about their body and food and withdrawing from social
  activities.

- Obsessive exercise and often anger if not able to exercise.

- Losing pleasure in previously pleasurable activities.

Bulimia

Bulimia is a condition that again too affects both males and
females and manifests as a combination of binge eating (over
eating and a feeling of loss of control over eating) usually on
high kilojoule foods, but it can be 'healthy foods', followed by
attempts to compensate for this eating by trying to get rid of
the food and calories. This compensatory behaviour can be in
the form of over-exercising, vomiting or periods of strict
dieting. The binge eating is eating a much larger quantity of
food than someone else would under the same conditions and

its often done in secret. Binge eating occurs once a week. It makes the person feel anxious, out of control, shameful and guilty and so the engagement in compensatory behaviours is aimed at trying to reduce these feelings and feel 'OK' again. As with anorexia, this behaviour is due to an unhealthy obsession with shape, weight and size. The compensatory behaviours are very dangerous often leading to dental damage, heart, lung, kidney and other organ complications as well as dehydration, lethargy and fatigue.

Some of the signs of bulimia in a child might be:

- Being emotional over eating and food.

- Being preoccupied with food and eating.

- Burst blood vessels or swelling of the face due to vomiting.

- Dental damage often noticed by a dentist due to the acid in vomit.

- Lethargy and fatigue due to loss of nutrients and dehydration.

- Going to the toilet straight after eating, often to get rid of the food.

- Finding wrappers or food hidden in the bedroom.

- Depression and anxiety over food.

- Over exercising and sometimes in secret.

Binge eating disorder

This is a condition where a person binge eats large qualities of food, often high calorie, in a discrete period of time, usually several times a week or month without engaging in compensatory behaviours. The reasons for binging are usually due to either a period of strict dieting where a person becomes over hungry or has something off their 'bad' list and therefore feels they've 'blown' their 'diet' or overeating for emotional reasons. The person feels out of control in their eating and it is very distressing.

Treatment for binge eating involves learning to relax when eating and slow it down. In schools and at home you can help a child by creating a relaxed atmosphere free from distraction during meal times. Schools often have lunch break where children have to sit for a certain period of time and finish their lunch before they can go play. This puts some control over eating and helps children focus on their food. At home, eating at the table, without distraction, is the most helpful. You can role model this yourself in front of your children by having family dinner and sitting down at breakfast and lunch. Rather than eating on the run.

Signs of binge eating include:

- Not eating in front of others.

- Eating very quickly.

- Eating in secret.

- Repeatedly continuing to eat even though they're full and being seemingly unable to stop eating.

- Finding empty wrappers of food.

- Distention in the stomach and appearing over full.

- An unhealthy focus on food.

- Preoccupation on food at social events such as children preferring to eat rather than play.

- Eating with hands instead of utensils (unless this is due to cultural reasons).

Talking about eating disorders

For teachers and counsellors talking to young people about eating disorders the questions below can be helpful in starting a discussion:

- What are the different disorders and who are affected by them?

- What are the dangers of eating disorders? This information is easily found on National Eating Disorder websites.

- What's healthy eating?

- What can you do to relax when eating (i.e., focused eating without distraction)?

- What can you do to feel better about yourself?

- Who can you talk to?

- There is treatment available and people to help (see the Appendix for services in your area or look up online).

What causes an eating disorder?

There are many causes of eating disorders but the biggest cause is body dissatisfaction. Body dissatisfaction may arise due to teasing, being overweight as a child, dieting, watching others dieting or restricting their intact, watching carers respond to emotions with eating, a family history of an eating disorder, playing certain sports that emphasise weight, size or shape (i.e., ballet, gymnastics, modelling), succumbing to media pressure to look a certain way, among many others causes. No one factor though is solely to blame. If you are aware of any of these factors in your life though, as an adult, work on role modelling positive behaviours around your own size, shape, weight and diet. The most important thing is to be a positive role model, ensure your child has someone to go to for support and recognise early warning signs so you can get help if needed.

How to help if you suspect a child or young person has an eating disorder

The most important thing is to be there to listen and help non-judgmentally and get them help from a professional. Don't try to change their eating without getting professional help as this can often make children and young people angry or anxious. Tell them you will help them get the help they need and they are not alone. If you have an eating disorder, make sure you are getting help for yourself. You must not blame yourself though. Do your best to be the best role model you can be and if you're concerned about your child and your behaviour in front of them, work on changing it today. Follow Chapter 3 on positive role modelling in terms of how you talk about food, weight, and appearance. There is a lot of professional help out there in terms of local eating disorder centres, doctors, specialist psychologists and counsellors, nutritionists and dieticians.

Class Activity: Eating disorders

A great activity to engage students around educating them about eating disorders is to talk about what they know about them and correct misunderstanding. It is probably best to separate boys and girls to do this exercise as they will have different ideas. For boys, focus more on muscle dysmorphia. But it is important for girls to look at the issues for boys too. It's best to dedicate a whole lesson to this. Having a teacher and counsellor present is a good idea when presenting this lesson so you can best respond to students' concerns about eating disorders.

You can introduce the activity by stating: *today we're going to look at the topic of eating disorders. These are serious conditions that affect young people. They include concerns over weight and shape to the point where the person goes to extreme efforts to try and control their eating and body.*

Explain briefly what the different disorders are and dispel myths such as eating disorders only affect girls, you have to be underweight to have an eating disorder, and so on. Talk about eating disorders affecting a person's thoughts about themselves including poor self-concept, body shape and size, perceptions about physical attraction, and depression. That dieting is the major cause of eating disorders but what are some others? Go through here, family, culture, media, and teasing influences. What you're aiming to do is to help students realistically assess their body image and weight and health management practices.

Next dispel myths of ideal body types like you did in previous chapters (like Chapter 1 and Chapter 5) where students can look through magazines or the Internet and talk about what's real and what isn't and what's healthy and why and what isn't and why. Get them to look at both genders. Ask students about the dangers of trying to live up to these ideals in terms of their behaviour and the way they may feel about themselves.

Then ask what can they do to stay healthy and not give in to pressures to look a certain way. Write their ideas up. Always finish on a positive so get each student to write down what they love about their bodies and how they keep their bodies healthy. Examples might include: I have fun with friends, I exercise for fun, I eat a variety of foods.

Another idea is to get students into pairs where each student traces around the body of another and then they write down all the things they love about their body and the function of each part. Then their friends can contribute to this or take it home for family members to add to. What you're emphasising here is diversity and how everybody's body is unique and deserves to be valued.

Some questions to ask to get students thinking about eating disorders are:

- What is unhealthy about female and male media models?
- What are the dangers of an over-emphasis on appearance including thinness and muscles?

- What are the dangers of using commercial weight loss products?
- What can be done to help people think about healthy body shape and size?
- How can you help a friend?
- Where do you get help from an adult?
- Who in the school can help?

At the end of the session ask student to write down what they have learned from this exercise and use this as a guide to stimulate discussion. At the end, provide a list of school and community resources for accessing help and where to go to for advice and assistance. Encourage them to share what they've learnt with their family. Also, finishing off with an exercise on self-esteem building is a positive way to finish up (see the end of Chapter 1, Chapter 10, and Chapter 11, for help with this).

Chapter summary

- Eating disorders are serious conditions affecting the mind and body.

- Eating disorders affect both genders.

- Eating disorders are more than just fussy eating.

- Look out for warning signs and communicate your concerns to the child or young person involved.

- Offer support and to help the child or young person find help.

- Research the services in your area.

- Take care of yourself as a helper.

CHAPTER 9

What's mental health and how do I get some of that?

I suffer from depression and sometimes I have really bad times where I can't go to work and stay in bed. My girls worry about me and they talk to my wife about it sometimes, especially my youngest who's 10. She doesn't understand but my 15 and 17 year old seem to have more awareness about depression as they've been taught about it at school. I have a clinical psychologist I go to who helps me and I'm on medication. My 'unwell' times are getting shorter and shorter which is great, so I'm getting there. But I know it's hard on my family at times. I'm glad that the school my girls go to teaches them about mental health and wellbeing and they have a counsellor they talk to at school. She's been a real help. I do worry about my girls 'getting depression', so I try real hard to stay healthy and also communicate openly with them about what helps to build my own resilience. — *Jonathon, 51*

This chapter covers the topic of mental wellness explaining what it is and how to promote it with children and young people. It covers the key areas of a person's life that need to be looked after including physical health, with strategies for talking to children and young people including problem solving. Even though this chapter is written to assist you to help children and young people, you yourself can follow the suggestions in your own life to improve your own mental health. When we as adults are resilient, we're better able to help children. Even if it's a work in progress for you, looking after your own mental health will send a positive message to those children and young people in your care.

What is mental health?

When we talk about feeling well we mean not just being physically healthy but mentally healthy as well. When we're mentally healthy we feel good from an emotional point of view and we can go about our daily activities and interact well socially with others. Healthy children and young people are those who have both their physical and emotional needs met. Adults play a significant role in promoting mental health through their role modelling as well as their education. As an adult, you're also the one who may notice signs of poor mental health so this chapter aims to help you role model positive mental health as well as how to talk to children and young people about it and how you and professionals can help.

First, let's start with an activity you can use to educate children and young people about mental health. Start by asking what they think mental health is and correct and clarify. For example, some of the things children might say (and that you want them to say) are that mental health is:

- Being healthy in your head.
- Feeling happy, but not necessarily all the time.
- Enjoying yourself and your life.
- Having good friends and close family. (For those children who are having family issues focus on quality relationships they may have with teachers or non-related adults.)

- Being relaxed.

- Having fun.

- Enjoying school.

- Being healthy in your body.

- Feeling like you belong (i.e., to school, church, sport, family, and friends).

- Talking to someone who can help when you're sad or worried.

- Feeling sad sometimes.

- Worrying sometimes.

- Feeling angry sometimes but being able to control it.

- Sleeping well.

- Asking for help.

Dealing with emotions

Sometimes adults struggle to deal with the up and down emotions of children and young people. So here are a few tips. It's important to highlight to children and young people that it's okay not to be happy all the time. That it's okay to feel a range of emotions in response to life events. Sometimes we will feel sad, for example, when something sad happens, and this is okay. It's normal, for example, for children to be very upset when a pet dies, when they fall out with their friends, when their sport team loses or when they get disappointed. It's also okay to be angry sometimes when something or someone annoys you. So normalise an array of emotions.

Stating how you yourself are feeling and why will help educate them too. Don't try and hide your emotions. Acknowledging your own feelings models acceptance of feelings in children. At the same time, be mindful of how you express certain emotions such as anger. Anger should never be expressed through physical or verbal violence. Sometimes children and young people express their sadness by being angry or irritated. This is okay as a child tries to process what's happened, as long as the anger is not expressed with violence. It's your job to help them express emotions in healthy ways. For example, going for a walk when you're angry or talking to someone about what is bothering you, or going somewhere quiet when you need time out.

What's important with emotions is how quickly a child bounces back after something has happened. This is often called *resilience* where children and young people feel all the emotions when different things happen, but are able to calm down and be okay relatively quickly. Resilience is also being able to problem solve and seek help. Building resilient children and young people involves helping them manage emotions, manage change, know when to seek help and who to ask, as well as being proud of themselves and their efforts and achievements. Praising a child or young person's efforts no matter what the achievement is a good way to help build resilience because they focus on doing and being involved in things rather than having to always 'win'. Doing their best needs to be encouraged and helping children realise that they can't be the 'best' at everything. That being happy for others and their successes is also important. For parents and carers, showing that you love them for who they are, not what they achieve, is important so children learn to appreciate their own individuality as well as that of others.

Young people and mental health

When talking to adolescents about mental health in particular, it's important to remember that this is an especially difficult time in life as so many changes to their body are happening as well as them trying to work out 'who they are' and forming an *identity* that they're happy with. Normalise this time of 'safe' experimentation and change that everyone goes through. Reminding them where they can go for help is important particularly given this time can be a time where adolescents may engage in risk taking behaviour that puts them at risk of harm. It's not unusual for adolescents to experiment with drugs and alcohol and they may start to engage in sexual activity. This is especially tricky for most parents and carers but it is okay to say 'no' to this behaviour and educate your child about protective behaviour, how to say no, how to stay safe and that you are there to help them.

Sometimes adolescents are more comfortable talking to older siblings, other adults (i.e., doctors, youth workers, family friends), and teachers, rather than parents, so make sure your child has someone you trust to talk to. Remember, you decide as a family, what the rules are around behaviour and what you role model as 'acceptable' behaviour. For example, as a parent or carer, you will need to consider how you role model drug and alcohol use, healthy eating, physical activity, screen time, sleep hygiene, communication and quality time.

Class Activity: Identity

This is an activity that can sometimes help clarify for a young person who they are and help them with identity formation. Ask the class to write down the answers to these questions:

- What do I like and what don't I like?

- What am I good at?

- What different roles do I have (i.e., student, daughter, neighbour, community member, and employee)?

- Who's in my life?
- What do I want to be when I grow up?
- What do I value?
- What is important to me?

How parents and carers can promote good mental health in young people

> I'm a father of three girls so there are four women in the house! Trying to manage this at times can be a real challenge and sometimes they gang up on me as a male. But it's all in jest. I take my girls to their sport training and events and cheer on the sidelines. Although my eldest, who's 17, would never admit it, as it's not 'cool' to have your dad there, she loves me being there. We go out for ice cream afterwards and she tells me all about her friends. It's a great time for the two of us to catch up.
> — Mario, father

Obviously you want the best for your child and to make their transition into adolescence as smooth as possible. But it can be a difficult, frustrating and worrying time for even the best of parents and carers. You're often dealing with mood changes (sometimes several throughout the day), a change from them listening and taking advice from you to listening to peers or the media, engagement in risky behaviour, lying, experimenting with drugs and alcohol, refusing to do chores or turn off their devices, among other things that worry us as adults. Make sure you're talking to your own friends and family with adolescent children to help normalise the experience and get support. Also, knowing who you can go to for help is important. There are many professionals who specialise in adolescent mental health such as local youth services.

Studies show a strong link between the quality of parent/carer–child relationships and young people's mental health but it can be a struggle at times to ensure healthy family relationships. Adolescents are wanting to become more independent, work out who they are and they often don't want to listen to adult 'advice'. The best way to help your adolescent is to ensure open communication and being available to them to help answer questions, correct misunderstandings, normalise their experience, help them with friendships and encourage healthy behaviours. Role modelling positive behaviours including help seeking is also important. This will reduce the chances of your child experiencing mental health problems as they know they have your unconditional support. Here are some ideas to promote mental health and wellbeing in the children and young people in your care. The term 'your child' is used here and defined as any child you're caring for.

- Show love, affection and care for your child as well as for others, role modelling emotional support. This might involve doing fun activities together, going to watch them play sport, giving cuddles, listening and not judging, being genuinely interested in what they're doing, and being available.

- Value their achievements and their efforts no matter how small. Praising 'having a go' for example, is more important than 'winning' at something. Also, help your child manage disappointment by naming it and helping them feel okay.

- Show that you're interested in what is happening in your child's life (even when they talk about things you might not be interested in). Especially for adolescents, they will often talk about their peers or social media that you might find annoying or unimportant, but recognise that it might be important to your child, so share in their stories.

- Encourage your child to have positive peer interactions, as this is associated with higher self-esteem. Teach them about making friends, how to tell what's a good friend and how they can be assertive when needed.

- Praise your child's character and their kindness towards others including animals, siblings, friends, and strangers. Doing this from an early age helps your child establish the importance of kindness to others and makes them less likely to be antisocial.

- Value your child's ideas and opinions. Remember they are trying to make sense of the world so they may challenge your ideas and values but this is all part of growing up. Try not to get defensive, acknowledge their point of view, and agree to disagree at times.

- Enjoy spending time together one-on-one with your child, and also as a family. This makes you more likely to know what is going on with your child. Eating dinner together for example is a great way for everyone to catch up with what each other is doing.

- Try and reduce screen time as this can distract you and your child from communicating with each other. Spending quality time where you communicate face to face is incredibly important to healthy relationship building.

- Set rules and boundaries. Even though adolescents may push the boundaries, they respond better to predictability and knowing the rules and family values. These will change depending on the age of your child so be open to change but also what you are and are not willing to negotiate on. A strong 'no' to drugs and alcohol, for example.

- Make punishment reasonable. Think about what is an appropriate punishment given your child's age and never ever use physical punishment or put downs. At the same time, there must be rewards and praise to keep punishment in balance.

- Be there for your child. Encourage your child to talk about feelings with you. It's important for your child to feel they don't have to go through things on their own, and that you can work together to find solutions to problems.

- Deal with problems as they arise, rather than letting them build up. Don't hold grudges or unreasonably long punishments, as this will make your child less likely to tell you when something doesn't go right.

- Reduce conflict in the home. If you and your partner are experiencing relationship issues, seek professional help. Children are aware when their parents/carers are unhappy and fighting so it's important to get this under control.

- Seek help for yourself if you are suffering from a mental health condition or going through a particularly stressful or challenging time. If you're in good physical and mental health, your child is more likely to be too. At the same time, don't beat yourself up if you are struggling. Get the help you need.

- If you have any concerns, talk to family members, friends, other parents or teachers. If you feel you need more help, speak to your local doctor, the school, or a health professional.

Being physically healthy

Given the connection between physical and mental health, where better physical health is associated with better mental health, let's look here in more detail about how to ensure the physical health of a child in your care.

When a child has a healthy body this helps their brain develop and helps them cope better with let downs and life's ups and downs. When a child is getting enough sleep, is eating well, is active, has friends, and goes to school, they are more resilient. As well, children need to be having regular dental, eye and physical check-ups to make sure their body is developing as best as it can. To help your child stay emotionally and physically healthy, encourage your child in the following habits.

Keep active

Physical fitness will help your child stay healthy, have more energy, feel confident, manage stress, sleep well and have a more positive body image. If your family is an active one, then your child is more likely to see physical activity as an important part of a healthy life. So switch off from electronics and go out and play, take the dog for a walk, walk to the shops, run around, and encourage sport participation. The World Health Organization recommends that children need to be physically active for at least 60 minutes per day. This helps them maintain a healthy body weight, have a healthy heart and lungs, develop strong bones, keep muscles and joints healthy and develop control over movement and coordination. This physical activity doesn't have to be structured exercise, just something that gets the body moving and its better if it's fun. Standing up instead of sitting for example, walking instead of driving, playing games outside instead of in, just to name a few.

Eat healthy and drink water

Develop and maintain healthy eating and drinking habits and role model healthy behaviours yourself. As we've talked about in previous chapters, role modelling positive eating behaviours yourself is important such as eating fresh foods that have a supportive function in your body. Children who eat healthy are far less likely to suffer from overweight and obesity, eating disordered behaviour and poor body image.

Sleep well

Get lots of regular sleep with stable bedtime and wake times. Quality sleep and routine will help your child to manage a busy life, stress and responsibilities of school, home and community life. If your child is not sleeping or sleeping too much, and it's not due to too much screen time, see your GP for help. Having rules around use of devices before bed need to be implemented so that children are 'switching off' before bed. Young children need anywhere between 10 to 12 hours of sleep and older children need between 8 to 12 hours. Good sleep hygiene is important, including switching off and relaxing before bed (i.e., listen to music, read a story), not eating or drinking or using stimulants too close to bedtime, not using devices before bed (the light stimulates the brain), only using the bed for sleeping (so the brain can associate bed with sleep and not tossing and turning or stress). If you (or your child) are having difficulties sleeping, doctors and psychologists can help with sleep hygiene.

Avoid drugs and alcohol

Talk to your child about the dangers of drugs and alcohol and role model healthy behaviour yourself. It's important to realise that as children go through adolescence, they might experiment with alcohol and drugs. You need to be open to talking about this with your child and try and be calm about it so they're more likely to come and talk to you. Taking drugs and using alcohol puts your child at a higher risk of developing mental health problems as well as physical harm to their growing body. You should encourage your child to avoid drugs and alcohol, and not provide opportunities for them to 'experiment'. Sometimes parents and carers think it's okay for their child to experiment with alcohol for example, in the family home. This sends a message that drinking is okay.

Think about your child's health and the effects of alcohol on the body. If you think your child is using drugs or alcohol and you're worried, talk with your child. Also consider speaking to a health professional, youth worker, school or counsellor.

Some signs a child in your care might need help

Just like adults, it's normal for children and young people to sometimes have low moods, be angry, lack motivation, be tired, not want to do certain things, and have trouble sleeping. It's not always the sign of a mental health problem. But if you do notice some of the following signs and they persist for more than a few weeks, especially for no obvious reason, it's important to seek help. Talking to your child regularly about how they're going is important so you're *tuned into* your child and you can recognise warning signs early. Take what they say seriously. As well, listen to what others around you might be saying as well as comments from your child's friends. Let's look here at some of the warning signs of mental health concerns for younger children and then young people.

Younger children

Sometimes we can misattribute a child's disobedient behaviour as them being 'naughty' but it may be a sign they're not coping. Some of the signs of the need to be concerned or get help in younger children might be if a child in your care is:

- Not engaging in things they used to enjoy.
- Seeming sad or unhappy much of the time.
- Saying that they feel sick or in pain for no obvious reason.
- Being more clingy than usual.
- Not performing as well at school academically.

- Receiving comments from others about a change in behaviour or learning.

- Having ongoing worries or fears or seeming to be stressed.

- Having problems fitting in at school or getting along with other children.

- Being aggressive or consistently disobedient, getting into trouble or having repeated temper tantrums.

- Having sleep problems, including nightmares that seem to be ongoing.

- Not eating or seems to have lost their appetite or the reverse, has started overeating or seeming to be eating to 'cope'.

Young people

It can be tricky with young people to decipher what is normal adolescent behaviour and what you need to be concerned about. You're really looking for sudden changes in behaviour that is out of character. Following are some of the things to look out for and when you may need to seek support and help. For example, if you notice the following in a young person in your care in addition to the ones listed before for younger children:

- Being moody much of the time without obvious reason.

- Not wanting to hang out with friends and avoiding social occasions.

- Being overly concerned with their appearance (more so than you would expect, as remember that during adolescence young people are usually more preoccupied with their appearance than at other stages) such as not wanting to leave the house due to their skin or body concerns.

- Lacking motivation to do things especially those they used to enjoy.

- Having trouble coping with everyday activities.

- Showing sudden changes in behaviour, often for no obvious reason.

- Having trouble eating or sleeping.

- Refusing to play sport.

- Attention seeking in both positive and negative ways (its important here to try and work out what your adolescent is trying to tell you as often they may be after more love and support by doing things that draw your attention to them).

- Dropping school performance, or suddenly refusing to go to school.

- Making comments about being in pain regularly (for example, headache, stomach ache or backache).

- Being aggressive or antisocial (e.g., missing classes at school, stealing or hurting others).

- Being very anxious about weight or physical appearance.

- Weight loss or failing to gain weight as they grow.

- Taking drugs or alcohol.

- Self-harm (deliberately injuring the body or causing pain to oneself). This requires professional help immediately. It's often a shock to parents and carers so seek help for yourself too.

- Talking about suicide. This needs to be taken very seriously and get help from a professional immediately. If your child seems to be in immediate danger call emergency or take them to hospital.

Talking with children and young people about mental health

If you're concerned about a child or young person's mental health, start by talking to them alone. Don't wait thinking the problem might go away. It isn't always easy to talk to a child or young person so here are some tips from the research on communicating with children and young people and encouraging a child or young person in your care to talk to you about how they're feeling. If you're a counsellor or youth worker you're probably already doing this but here are some tips to check:

- State that you're worried and you want to help. The child may at first refuse to talk but just let them know you're there to support them when they're ready and that everyone has worries and troubles, including you. Tell the child or young person that talking about a problem can often help solve it or lesson the burden. That together, you can try and work through or solve the problem.

- Ask them if they would like some help from you or someone else and don't be upset if they'd prefer to talk to someone else. Help them find someone else to talk to that you're comfortable with. Offer to go with them to seek professional help. State that talking to professionals is normal and smart and that everyone needs someone to talk to who can help.

- Try not to get embarrassed or upset by what the child or young person tells you. Try and remain calm and listen non-judgmentally. This makes them more likely to come talk to you again in the future when there's a problem.

- Acknowledge that opening up about personal thoughts and feelings can be scary but that you won't judge them or laugh at them and that you'll take them seriously and try your best to help.

- Let the child know that talking with a doctor, school counsellor, youth worker, or psychologist is confidential and someone they can trust. That often they're better equipped to help than those that are close to us because they can be more objective and also they're specifically trained in helping children and young people.

- If you're a counsellor or teacher, you will need to talk about the limits of confidentiality and that if you're concerned you may need to talk to their carers, but that you'll do this together and with support.

- If you're a parent or carer, role model listening behaviour by showing your child you listen to their siblings, your partner, and your friends.

- Give them the numbers and websites to go to for a confidential chat to a professional if appropriate.

- Make sure you get help for yourself. Supporting a child or young person can be challenging so make sure you are okay and you have someone to debrief to if needed. For counsellors and health professionals, make sure you have a supervisor to assist you with tricky situations particularly if you're worried about a child and/or their carer.

Positive role modelling and mental health stigma

Remember that as an adult, it's important that you role model healthy mental health and wellbeing through your actions. So make sure you are looking after yourself. Finding time to relax, doing things you enjoy, eating healthy, exercising, staying away from drugs and alcohol, as examples. Make comments to children and young people about what you're doing and why. For example, I'm going for a walk to enjoy the fresh air and make my body feel good. I'm doing my hobby because I love it and it relaxes me. I'm going to talk to my friend for their different perspective on my problem etc.

There's no shame in asking for help but many people reluctantly seek help from professionals, thinking there's negative stigma attached to help seeking. In reality, when a person asks for help they've recognised there's a problem and made a decision to solve it or at least make it better. They've used a problem solving approach and that's smart. Sometimes we can battle with problems for months or even years before we seek help, and often when we finally do seek help it is great and we wonder why we didn't do it before. Here's a list of a few places to go for help. You may like to give this list to your students if you're a teacher or counsellor.

Where to go for help:

- School teacher or school counsellor or pastoral care person.

- Your parents or carers.

- A trusted adult friend or family member.

- Your coach.

- Your doctor.

- Youth services in your area (provide numbers or web sites to students).

- Kids help lines in your area (provide numbers or web sites to students).

- Australian/American/British Psychological Society (to find a psychologist who can help).

- Mental health services in your capital city for confidential telephone or web services.

- Eating disorder foundations in your city.

- Nutritionist/dietician.

- Women's or men's health centres.

- Paediatrician or child health centre.

There are also lots of smartphone apps for children and young people that can help with relaxation, managing anxiety and depression, talking to friends, dealing with anger, just to name a few. Provide some examples in class to your students so they can see what's available to them.

In the Appendix of this book there are lists of services to assist in your area.

Class Activity: Talking about help seeking

A great classroom activity is to have a lesson on help seeking. Talking to children and young people about help seeking and why it's important, as well as where to go for help, increases the chances they will ask for help. Talk to the class about who you are (if you're a counsellor or pastoral care person) and how they can seek out your help (i.e., how to book to see you, room location, office hours). Talk about how we all need help at times in our lives. After introducing the lesson on mental health and what it is (see above), you could ask the class for some of the reasons why someone might not ask for help or what they might be worried about and then comment on why or why not that's true with the aim of increasing the likelihood they will ask for help. Some of the reasons they might come up with for not asking for help or concerns they have are following, as well as what you might say back:

- *You're weak if you ask for help.* No-one can solve all their problems alone and knowing you need to ask for help, including asking for help for others, makes you a smart person. Others can offer insight, support, normalise the problem as well as help you solve it more quickly.

- *I'll lose control of my emotions if I ask for help such as crying, getting upset or angry.* Sometimes young people are embarrassed to cry in front of others or talk about feelings. It's normal to feel this way and remember that people won't judge you harshly for showing emotion. You may have to talk here about choosing the 'right' person for help and not giving up help seeking if the first person they talk to isn't that helpful.

- *Will I be expected to return the favour if I ask for help as I might not be able to do that?* Talk to children and young people about how most people do not expect this, especially adults. Often asking for help increases the trust between you and your friend because it gives us permission to talk about feelings and find solutions. Also, others often feel good when they can help us. There are also specific people at school there to offer help.

- *Won't asking for help burden my friend or family member?* Emphasise here that it's important to go to the right person for help. Often friends are great at just hearing out the problem we're experiencing and comforting us but they may not know the answers. This is okay, as a friend, you can just listen and offer to help your friend find the right person to help. Adults can help us problem solve the solutions to our concerns that our friends might not be able to. They have more experience solving problems remember. Emphasise here too that if they're worried about a friend, they should seek adult help.

- *How do I know when to talk to a friend vs an adult?* Talk to the class about how they can help each other. Maybe even brain storm with the class when they can go to their friend for help and when to go to an adult. For example, if you're a school counsellor, you might talk about the sorts of problems children and young people come to you for and how you've helped them.

- *What is a counsellor or psychologist?* Most children (and adults) don't know what different professionals do and why you'd go to one person vs another so educate them about what different professionals specialise in and how they can help. State that they are trained to help with mental health and wellbeing, its confidential, how you can make an appointment, whether they need parental permission, and so on.

- *I'm used to solving problems on my own.* Some young people are used to having to solve problems on their own particularly if they don't have trusted adults in their lives at home. Talk about the benefits of asking for help and use examples.

- *Will I get in trouble if I ask for help or tell an adult what I'm doing?* Children and young people often worry that if they ask an adult for help they'll get in trouble particularly if they think they've done something wrong. So it's important as an adult, especially a parent, that you listen, praise the child for asking for help, and offer a solution without judgement or punishment. Young people are usually especially worried if they've done something they're not allowed to do such as use drugs or alcohol. Tell them to be brave and to trust an adult to help. As a counsellor, you may also need to state to parents and carers the need to be calm when talking about these things and be pleased their child told them rather than being angry.

- *Will you have to tell my parents?* Remind students about who is in your school to talk to confidentially and reassure them that this person or persons are going to make things as easy as possible. That yes, sometimes parents need to be involved but that the child's confidentially will be respected as much as possible. That usually the issue has to be quite serious to have to involve parents. Make sure you are clear on the policies around informed consent and confidentiality.

A good follow up to this activity is sending something home to the parents and carers of children so they know what's been covered in your lesson. This increases the chances of parents and carers having open conversations with their child about mental health and well-being. It will also provide them with directions of where to go for extra help.

What's unhelpful help seeking?

It's important to talk here about what is not helpful in terms of help seeking. Ask the class what wouldn't be helpful if you had a problem? Some of the suggestions might be:

- Hoping the problem will just go away.
- Talking to someone I don't trust.
- Talking to friends in a large group.
- Staying silent.
- Not telling adults for fear of their reaction.
- Stewing over a problem.

- Using drugs or alcohol to cope.
- Avoiding the situation (like not going to school).

By the end of the class activity, ensure that students know where they can go to get help. Talk about which teachers they can go to, how to contact the school counsellor and other support people such as a chaplain, pastoral care teacher or parents. Also, normalise help seeking even giving an example where you have asked for help and how it was helpful.

Class Activity: Problem solving

Here's an activity to do with students that involves an example of troubleshooting how to help a fellow student. You can change the gender or age depending on the students you are conducting the lesson with.

> Sam is 13 years old and she is being teased by her peers. She feels alone and like no-one understands what she's going through. She doesn't want to say anything because she's embarrassed and she's also worried she'll be seen as a tattle tailer by her peers if she tells an adult.

Ask the students these questions:

- *What would you say to Sam to help her?*
  Here you want students to talk about what a friend would do (i.e., listen, comfort, reassure). Some good responses to these questions are: listen to her, offer to come with her to see the school counsellor or a teacher. Use the suggestions mentioned in previous sections to assist as well as talking about friendship and how friends can help.

- *What else might help Sam?*
  Here you want students to think about how other people might help (i.e., talking to a teacher, a parent). Encourage students, even if they feel overwhelmed by one of their friend's problems, it's okay to encourage their friend to seek adult help.

Remind students of unhelpful ways to cope. Highlight the importance of not taking on the problem alone especially if their friend is in danger or doing something harmful (i.e., self-harm or drug and alcohol use).

Chapter summary

Talking to children and young people about the importance of help seeking and educating them about why, when, and who to ask for help is important for looking after their overall wellbeing. Remember too that being a helper can be draining and so you need to seek your own person to debrief and listen to you. Seek professional help yourself too if you need it. In summary:

- Look out for warning signs that a child or young person is having troubles.

- Be open to talking to children and young people about mental health and wellbeing in a calm and helpful manner.

- Normalise help seeking and worries and troubles and emphasise the benefits of talking to someone. There's no need to be embarrassed, so role model help seeking yourself.

- Realise that the child in your care may prefer to talk to someone else whom they trust.

- Seek help for yourself and the child if needed.

- Role model positive mental and physical health.

- Adults are best at helping with tricky problems.

- Children and young people need to know where to go to seek help so provide in writing, names, numbers, and websites.

- This chapter's activities often follow well after Chapter 7 on bullying and body bashing, followed by Chapter 10 on general wellbeing.

CHAPTER 10

Relaxation and fostering positive emotions in yourself and others

Every night my daddy tucks me in before I go to sleep and gets me to think about my relaxing place, free from worries and troubles. I think about when we went on holidays to the beach over school holidays and I played in the water and on the sand. We built sand castles including one where the mermaid was living. She was protected by water around the castle and she was safe. I think about being that princess where no-one can harm her, she's enjoying the sand and the sun and going for a swim when she wants to. She swims in the ocean and loves looking at the fish and the rocks. My daddy says 'good night my princess' and kisses me on my forehead and I go to sleep. Sometimes, when I'm worried, my daddy reminds me that like the mermaid, I can swim off my worries and troubles and my daddy is looking out for me. — *Elizabeth, 7*

This chapter is all about how to help children and young people foster positive mental health through specific scientifically valid practices. We will go through mindfulness, visualisation, relaxation, engagement in pleasant activities and fostering gratitude. I'd encourage you, as a responsible adult in children and young people's lives, to engage in these practices yourself if you're not doing so already. It will help you foster wellbeing and health. Part of being a good role model is demonstrating to children and young people in your life that you can relax, do enjoyable things, take time out for yourself, appreciate the small things and have fun. Then they are more likely to copy. Let's start by talking about mindfulness.

Mindfulness — for you and the children and young people in your care

Mindfulness is increasing in popularity as a way to teach being focused on the simple present moment to assist with relaxation, calming, focusing on the present rather than worrying about the past or future, and general mental wellbeing. It involves focusing your attention on internal (i.e., feeling warm) or external (i.e., what you can hear) experiences in the present moment of time without passing judgement, just accepting it's there and you're aware of it. For example, really focusing on the one task such as feeling the breeze outside, doing a puzzle, enjoying sand running through your fingers, enjoying every mouthful of food. It has been found to be an effective practice for treating stress, anxiety, depression, eating disorders, body image, and physical and mental health. Children who engage in mindfulness have been found to be better at concentrating and attending, increasing memory, increasing pleasant feelings, assisting with sleep, relaxing, among many other benefits. It's about concentrating on the one task and what you're doing, without distractions. Children are often particularly good at focusing on the one task such as really getting into playing a game. Little children, for example, might enjoy brushing their doll's hair and focusing on how it feels without distraction.

Can you think of some times when you are truly in the moment without distraction? It's hard. How many times, for example, have you been driving to a destination and not remembered the journey at all because you were focusing on something else? Well if you're being mindful you're focusing on everything that you're doing at that time and place. Even if it's just for a few minutes, mindfulness can be a great tool for focusing and relaxation.

Mindfulness takes practice and it can be frustrating as we try to block out other thoughts and focus on what we're doing. But it's about allowing your thoughts to just flow in and out whilst trying to draw your attention to what you're doing. Have a practice with things like the washing up, thinking about how the water feels on your skin, or the sounds you're making, or how the dishes feel, and not worry about anything else. This is mindfulness, where you're focused on the present, what you're doing, and not judging yourself. Or sitting outside and thinking about what you can hear, see, feel, smell and even taste.

Being able to concentrate on the one thing makes us truly present. Mindfulness is often used to assist with *binge eating*, for example, where the person is asked to really focus on the taste, texture and pleasure of eating the one food without rushing. You can do such an activity with your child over snack or meal times where you both focus on what you can taste, smell, feel, see and even hear (like the crunching sounds eating makes). Really appreciating the moment. It's an active process where we chose to focus our attention on the present. Another activity around mindful eating is about giving the class raisons or a small lolly or treat and asking them to savour the taste and eat it as slowly as possible, really focusing on its smell, taste, texture, and so on. This can help those children especially who may be eating too quickly, such as the case might be in binge eating.

Try this simple exercise where you're focusing on relaxing. Go to a quiet place where you might lie down and close your eyes and just simple 'be' where you focus on your senses such as how your body feels, what you can hear, what you can feel, what you might be able to smell or even taste.

In the classroom, mindfulness is often used to help children calm down and concentrate. For example, when you're trying to calm a class after lunch or play time. You might ask the children to close their eyes and sit quietly and focus on the sounds, smells, and feelings going on around them. Thinking about how their body might feel in their chair or their heart beating or their breathing. This often brings children into the present, calms them down and gets them ready for the lesson ahead.

There are many, many, mindfulness apps to download to use to help children relax and sleep. Practise yourself just bringing your attention to the here and now.

When you first start, you might find it frustrating as you can't 'switch off' or thoughts are interfering. Just try to ignore the thoughts and focus your attention on what you're doing. Try for a few seconds, then a minute, then more until you can work up to being mindful for 10 to 20 minutes. Try with different things such as lying down and closing your eyes and focusing on your breathe for a few minutes.

Visualisation

Another technique to induce calm and relaxation is to think of somewhere peaceful such as a beach, woods, forest, stream and the like. This is *visualisation* where we concentrate on something or somewhere that makes us feel relaxed. When we think about our relaxing place, focus on this being a safe, tranquil place. Where is it? What can you see? Hear? Feel? Touch? Smell? Taste? For example, a child might think about the last time they went to the beach and they can see the ocean, the birds, the sand, their sandcastle, and hear the ocean, the birds, children playing, they can smell the ocean, the fresh air, and feel the water, the sun, the sand etc. For teachers, you might like to guide your class in an activity of thinking about somewhere relaxing or somewhere that makes them happy and ask them to focus on the sights, sounds, smells, touch and tastes or give them a specific example to think of like being in a forest and seeing the trees, listening to the wind, smelling the flowers, tasting the rain, etc. Do this activity very slowly, for a few minutes, so children and young people, and yourself, can really get into it.

With older children and adolescents you might ask them to think of a place that they feel relaxed and comfortable. Or a memory of such a place. For example, being at a grandparent's place. What does it smell like? How does it feel? What can you see? Hear? Taste? This visualisation can be brought to mind whenever they need to relax like trying to sleep. You can do the same things, think of somewhere from your childhood where you felt safe and secure and bring in your senses to re-intact it in your mind.

Progressive muscle relaxation

As well as using mindfulness and visualisation, there are many structured relaxation strategies to teach children and young people how to relax. Progressive muscle relaxation is one method that helps children learn the difference between tension and relaxation in their body. This form of relaxation really helps them get in touch with their body and become aware of when they are tense and how to relax. Here is an example you can do with children in the classroom or at home. Children and adults often don't 'get' relaxation straight away, it takes practice and so do this a few times with children until they get the swing of it. You too will need to practise it so you can demonstrate to the children in your care. For children, it's easier to give instructions, getting them to imagine objects that they're holding or pretending to be animals stretching. For adolescents and adults you can use this script too but you might take out the reference to objects and animals.

Class or Home Activity: Relaxation

You might like to introduce the relaxation activity this way. Now we're going to practise a way to relax. This is really good when we feel tense or stressed or worried about something. Instruct children that in order for them to get the best feeling they must follow what you say. They might feel a bit silly but everyone is going to be doing it (including you). Just try and go with it and don't worry about doing it 'right' as there is no 'right' way. I'm going to ask you to pay attention to your body and how it feels, particularly how your muscles feel. Tell them you're going to go through each part of their body noticing tension and then relaxing each bit. We're going to start with our arms and hands and move all the way down to our toes and feet.

Adults and older adolescents can do this activity without using the analogies of fruit and animals and can just focus on tensing and relaxing the muscles. But for younger children it can often help to think about holding objects or being like an animal.

To start, instruct children to get comfortable in their chair or lying down, depending on how the classroom is set up or if you're doing this at home. If sitting, get them to sit back, put both feet on the floor, and let their arms hang loose. It's easier if they close their eyes. You may need to tell them not to laugh or look around the room at others. We've all got our eyes closed so no one is looking at anyone. Tell children that if they have any injuries, just miss the activity on that part of the body. If you know of any injuries that a specific child has, you may need to tell them discretely not to tense that part (i.e., back or neck injuries can be painful if tensed during this activity). When the class is settled tell them now we're going to begin.

This exercise has been adapted from many of the free relaxation scripts and apps for children available on the Internet. You might like to go through several with your child at home to see which one is best for them. Alternatively you can record yourself going through the exercise below for them to play later. It's good for everyone to practise relaxation and you yourself will find it easier to teach your child or children if you've practised it yourself first. There are many adult versions available for free. The best progressive muscle relaxation goes slowly so this activity should take about 15 minutes.

Relaxation script for children

Let's first start with the **hands and arms**. Say something like: Pretend you have two lemons in your hands. Now squeeze them hard like you're trying to squeeze out all the juice from them. Feel how tight your hand and arm are when you squeeze the lemon. Get them to pretend to squeeze it as hard as they can. Get them to do this for a few seconds. Now tell them to drop the lemon and notice how their muscles feel when they are relaxed. Letting their hands go, arms fall and just relax the muscles. Notice the difference between tension and relaxation. Now do it again, slowly. Pretend you've got another lemon in each hand and try and squeeze it again squeezing until all the juice is out. Now tell them to drop the lemons from both hands and relax. See how much better your hand and arm feel when they are relaxed. Wait a few seconds for them to notice the relaxation.

Next we're going to focus on our **arms and shoulders**. I want you to pretend you are a tired and lazy cat or dog. You want to stretch. Stretch your arms out in front of you. Then raise them up high over your head. Feel the pull in your shoulders and your back. Stretch higher. Hold this for a few seconds (judge this by practising on yourself beforehand). Now just let your arms drop back to your side. Then ask them to do this again so they really get a feel for the difference between being tense and being relaxed. Stretch your arms out in front of you. Then raise them over your head. Pull them back, way back. Pull hard. Now let them drop. Good. Notice how your shoulders and arms feel more relaxed. This time let's have a great big stretch. Try to touch the ceiling. Stretch your arms way out in front of you. Then raise them way up high over your head. Push them way, way back. Notice the tension and pull in your arms and shoulders and your back. Hold tight, now. Great. Let them drop and feel how good it is to be relaxed. It feels relaxed and not tense or stressed. Again, wait a few seconds before moving on to the next body part.

Remind children that they now have relaxed hands, arms and shoulders.

The next part is our **back**. Our back holds lots of tension supporting our bodies and we need to try and relax it. What I want you to do is squeeze your shoulder blades together and push your chest out and hold it there. Like you're trying to puff your chest out like a king or queen with your shoulders back, head up and chest out. Hold it there as tightly as you can (hold for a few seconds). Then let it go. Let your chest drop, shoulders drop, back relax. Focus on how much more relaxed your shoulders and your back feel. You might like to repeat.

You now have relaxed hands, arms, back, shoulders, and chest.

The next part of our body is our **face**. (Remember to go slowly.) We're going to tense our **jaw.** Pretend you have a giant hard round lolly in your mouth that's hard to chew. Bite down on it hard. Let your **cheek** and **neck** muscles help you. Chew it hard. Do this for a few seconds. Now relax. Just let your jaw hang loose. Notice how good it feels just to let your jaw drop. Let's try it again. Bite down hard on the lolly. Try to squeeze it out between your teeth. That's good. Now relax again. Just let your jaw drop. It feels good just to let go. Focus on how relaxed your whole body feels. Keep yourself as loose as you can.

Now we're going to focus on relaxing the rest of our **face**. Here comes a fly and it's landed on your **nose**. Try to get him off by wrinkling your nose and not using your hands. Make as many wrinkles in your nose as you can. Scrunch your nose up really hard. Good. Now you can relax your nose. Oh no he's come back again so wrinkle your nose again to try and get rid of him. Wrinkle it up hard. Hold it just as tight as you can. You'll notice your forehead and cheeks are tense too so stop wrinkling your nose and let your whole face relax.

Now we're going to focus on our **stomach**. Imagine that a tiny baby elephant is about to step on your stomach. So it doesn't hurt, make your stomach very hard by tightening up your stomach muscles and holding them tight as if you're bracing for the elephant. Hold it. He misses your body so you can relax now. Let your stomach go soft. Let it be as relaxed as you can. That feels so much better. Now tighten again as the baby elephant is coming back. Tight as you can. Nope, he's gone again so you can relax. Relax your muscles as you're safe and secure. No need to worry or be anxious. Just relax your whole body.

Remind children you now have relaxed hands, arms, back, shoulders, chest, face, and stomach.

Now pretend that you are at the beach (or in quick sand or mud) standing in heavy wet sand and your **feet** are covered in wet thick sand as they sink deeper and deeper into the sand. Squish your toes down deep into the sand. Try to get your feet down as far into the wet sand as possible. You will need your **legs** to help you. Push down, spread your toes apart, feel the wet sand squish up between your toes. Now step out of the wet sand and wriggle your toes. Relax your feet and legs. Let your toes go loose and feel how nice it feels to be relaxed and out of the heavy wet sand. Now try that again, put your feet back into the heavy wet sand and squish your toes down. Let your leg muscles help push your feet down. Push your feet. Hard. Now pull your feet out again. Relax your feet, relax your legs, and relax your toes. It feels so good to be relaxed. No tension anywhere. You feel nice and relaxed all over your body.

Remind children you now have relaxed hands, arms, back, shoulders, chest, face, stomach, feet and legs.

At the end

Tell the children to try and stay as relaxed as they can. Let your whole body go limp and feel all your muscles relaxed. In a few minutes I will ask you to open your eyes, and that will be the end of this practice session. As you go through the day, remember how good it feels to be relaxed. Sometimes you have to make yourself tighter before you can be relaxed, just as we did in these exercises. So during the day you can tense a part of your body for a few seconds and then release it, relax it. Practise these exercises every day to get more and more relaxed. A good time to practise is at night, after you have gone to bed and the lights are out and you won't be disturbed. It will help you get to sleep. You can also use it at school when you want to relax. Just remember the lemons, the cat, being a king or queen, the elephant, the fly or the heavy wet sand. Tense that part of your body and then relax it, feeling the difference between being tense and relaxed. You may even want to teach your friends, siblings, or an adult in your life.

Pleasant events scheduling

There is a wealth of research showing that in order to feel good and happy we need to be doing things we enjoy, or pleasant events. These can be anything from doing a hobby, playing with friends, reading, playing sport, spending time with loved ones, listening to music, just to mention a few. Doing things we enjoy helps reduce stress, increase wellbeing, reduces the chances of developing anxiety and depression, and promotes positive body image and healthy eating, among many other benefits. As adults, it's important we are role modelling time out for ourselves to enjoy life. If children see us having fun and enjoying life they are more likely to be happy too.

Children are great observers of adult behaviour so remember to lead by example. Often we say we're too tired, stressed, busy, and so on, to relax and unwind but it's important that we do this so we can cope with life events as well as role modelling to children that they need to have time out for enjoyment too. If you don't spend time relaxing, you can't be truly present and engaged in life. Rather, you're preoccupied with work, household chores, looking after others, which drains your body and mental health. You need to prioritise yourself so you have the energy and enthusiasm to look after others.

So write down a few things that you enjoy or help you relax and schedule when you're going to do them during the week. By scheduling relaxation and pleasure into our day, it makes us more likely to follow through with it.

Doing family activities are great ways to have fun with children and young people and to encourage closeness. This opens up the opportunity for communication and discussion of what is going on in a person's life. Also, children and young people are more likely to talk to us as adults whilst they're doing something else. For example, you can often get them to talk whilst you're in the car, playing a game or doing other enjoyable activities because they're more relaxed.

Often parents and carers think that young people won't want to hang out with them, but they do. It's often about choosing the activity carefully. For example, what does your child like doing and how can you do that with them? It might be shopping, playing sport, going to the movies, making food. Find out what your child likes doing and do it with them.

Class or Home Activity: Make a list of things you enjoy
As a class, you might like to ask children and young people to write a list of all the things they enjoy from things that take them a few minutes like listening to their favourite song, to things that take longer, like playing a team sport. This list is something they can refer to when they might be bored, stressed, down or wanting to just generally feel good. Then ask them to schedule it into their week. Being specific about what it is and when they're going to do it is important. Write yourself a list too and share it with your family.

Gratitude

Gratitude is about expressing appreciation for what we *have* as opposed to what we may *want*. Studies show that by increasing our feelings of gratitude, we can increase our happiness and wellbeing. It involves being thankful for what we have in life whether that be basic needs such as clean water to drink or higher needs such as being loved by others. It's something we can incorporate into our everyday life and try to truly focus

on it throughout the day. Appreciating what we have is important, especially comparing ourselves to those who have less.
That's not to say that we need to feel guilty about having
things others may not have, but it's about appreciating things
we have or the choices we have. For example, being able to
choose what school our children go to or choose what job we
do or choose how to spend our weekend. Other things might
be appreciating experiences with friends and family or having
opportunities to do fun things or achieving a goal.

We can teach our children to be grateful for their home, the
people that love them, the toys they can play with, and opportunity to go to school. We can educate them about families
who don't have choice and are fighting adversity or for people
who for certain cultural or religious reasons are treated poorly
or unfairly. Getting children to be kind to others and helping
others less fortunate also teaches gratitude. Asking what can
they do to help another today? And being thankful that they
have the ability to help.

Young people can often be quite consumed by themselves
and what is going on in their own lives and forget about
focusing on others less fortunate. As a class activity, it can be
a good reminder to ask what are they grateful for when they
look at the world around them or watch the news.
Appreciating the small things and the things we take for
granted. We too, as adults, need to remind ourselves of this
especially when we get wrapped up in and stressed about
things. Asking ourselves does it really matter on the grand
scale of things? Being grateful for what we have rather than
constantly searching for more or whining about what we don't
have. This is important to reduce stress by putting things in
perspective. Asking will this thing I'm stressing over be a big
deal still by this time next week? Getting young people especially to focus on their worries on a grander scale. Will my

worry about this pimple, this fight with my friend, still be an issue in one week?

When talking to children and young people about being grateful is important to point out the benefits including:

- It helps you worry less about the small things in life.

- It instantly boosts our mood and positive feelings towards our own life.

- It makes you enjoy life more because you appreciate things more.

- It makes you feel closer to those around you because you learn to appreciate them more.

- It helps your physical health because you'll be more likely to appreciate it and therefore take care of yourself.

- It helps you cope with life and stressful times by putting things in perspective.

- It makes other people feel good when we're thankful for what they do for us.

Personal Activity: Make a list of things for which you are grateful
What am I grateful for? Write some things down and keep adding to your list every day. You could keep a *gratitude journal* of things that happen to you that you're pleased about and write them down. Taking pictures is also another way to remember and keep track of things you're thankful for.
Some days it's easier to be more grateful than others and when we're struggling, getting out our list might help. Think about times gone by where you experienced something positive and were thankful for it. For example, it might be a good memory of something that you really enjoyed and you might be thankful for the experience. When you feel down you can revisit your gratitude journal and remind yourself of the good things in your life.

Telling others that they make you happy or you're glad that they're in your life, is also a way to express gratitude. It's important to express gratitude to others so they can benefit from the positive feelings people get from being thankful.

Class Activity: Gratitude

As a class, open the discussion about what is gratitude and what are students grateful for. Ask them to write some things down and share with their peers or the whole class. You could ask the students to make a poster each of things they're thankful for or make a special box to keep private gratitudes in that they can take home and keep adding to everyday. You may need to prompt students, in which case suggestions such as being grateful for a good laugh with a friend or a warm day might help. It doesn't have to be big things it can be really simple such as being thankful that you have an opportunity to learn or to see friends. They can go home and have a conversation with the family about what they're grateful for or at the dinner table, each person stating what they're grateful for today.

Chapter summary

So a combination of focusing on the here and now, trying to relax, doing things you enjoy and appreciating life is important to wellbeing. It will help children and young people worry less about appearance issues as they focus on their health overall and the needs of others. Seeing things in perspective is important and needs to be encouraged. This, as well as being physically healthy, getting enough sleep, eating nutritious food and engaging in regular exercise, will help children and young people stay healthy and happy.

All these benefit the body:

- Relaxation.

- Engagement in pleasant events.

- Being grateful for our life.
- Physical activity.
- Eating nutritious foods.
- Good sleep.
- Being close to friends and family.

CHAPTER 11

Concluding comments and guidelines for creating body image friendly schools

> I've been practising describing someone without using negative language around their appearance. For example, 'You know Stephanie, she's the teacher of the year two children who smiles a lot and has vibrant red hair and usually sits at the end of the table in staff meetings'. I try to stay clear of making comments about people's appearance in negative ways and correct people when they say things like, 'You know Bill, he's the funny looking man who teaches year ten'. Instead, 'You know Bill, he teaches the year tens and he recently helped with the school fete jumping castle'. — *Mandy, year 11 teacher*

We've talked a lot about positive role modelling and its importance in schools. Here is a list of summarised ways to make your school a body image friendly school with recommendations taken from research conducted on schools and government papers:

- Make celebrating and appreciating body diversity part of the school's mission statement.

- Say no to appearance-related teasing including having procedures to prevent and discourage cyberbullying such as antibullying policies.

- Make body image age appropriate education part of the curriculum and part of staff training.

- With primary school age children, teach them about positive body image, wellbeing, and respecting others.

- High school-aged students should be taught about appropriate peer interactions including handling bullying and media literacy.

- High school-aged students should also be taught about eating disorders and mental health and wellbeing.

- Where to go to access help at school and in the community is important for all ages.

- Make uniforms body image friendly with a variety of sizes and ranges to assist students to feel comfortable especially when it comes to sport.

- Make sure there is no weighing or weight, size and shape comparisons made between students in the class environment as this causes great distress to some students.

- Provide a nutritious variety of foods available in the school canteen/cafeteria.

- Provide many opportunities for students to engage in a wide range of sports and physical activities for different fitness levels, in a non-competitive, non-weight loss focused environment.

- Teachers must model positive body image through their actions and talk, and training be provided if possible, such as training in the use of body image friendly language (i.e., not using words with negative associations such as 'fat' when describing people).

- Train staff in the identification of students at risk of body image concerns and eating disorders.

- Have appropriate support staff for students and teachers.

To support parents and carers of school-aged children the school can do the following:

- Educate parents as to what the school's polices around body image and appearance teasing and bullying are.

- Provide parents with links to body image and eating disorder websites for information.

- Educate parents about the issues of body image and how they are being addressed at school and also how they can support their child.

- Have information nights for parents and carers around body image and eating issues.

- Educate parents and carers about positive role modelling.

- Educate parents and carers about where to go for additional help within and outside of the school.

Concluding comments

Being comfortable with your body and yourself is an ongoing process. Regularly checking in with yourself as to how you're feeling about your body and yourself is important. At any stage you can revisit the strategies you've learnt, to feel better and think more positively. We can learn how to appreciate our bodies more by listening to the innocence of young children and the way they talk about what their bodies do. Life is up and down and sometimes it's about riding the wave, going through ups and downs but being 'OK' overall. Being a positive role model to children and young people takes effort and time. Thinking about what you're doing and why and what the children and young people in your care may be thinking. Keep on educating yourself about body image and general wellbeing and mental health. Share your knowledge with other adults. We don't always get it right the first time but keep trying and get the help you need to do the best you can.

I wish you well in your own journey and in your journey with your children, friends, and families. Your dedication to helping others will not go unrecognised. Keep it up as together we can more positively influence the lives of children and young people.

Remember the following

- Body image is a perception of your body that you can change to be more positive.

- Our body image attitudes and beliefs influence how we feel and behave.

- There's no such thing as a perfect body.

- Everybody is beautiful in their own unique way.

- Body image changes as we age and develop.

- We can choose how we respond to the influences on our body image development with culture, peers, family and school being big influences.

- Children and young people look to us as adults for guidance on understanding themselves and their bodies.

- If we role model positive behaviours, our children are more likely to follow.

- Education helps children and young people understand themselves and the world.

- Mental wellbeing also involves good practices around physical health, good sleep, fun and play, positive work experiences, friendships, spirituality, love and respect for others and ourselves.

- Always be an active listener and try and remain calm and not judge.

- Always ask for help if you need it.

- Realise you are not alone in this journey.

All the very best on your educational journey, Vivienne.

Bibliography

Includes scientific papers, helpful books and government reports.

Any Body's Cool (2016). *Body image program for schools.* Produced by Mental Illness Education ACT.

Bertino, M.D., Richens, K., Knight, T., Toumbourou, J.W., Ricciardelli, L. & Lewis, A.J. (2013). Reducing parental anxiety using a family based intervention for youth mental health : A randomized controlled trial, *Open Journal of Psychiatry, 3*(1A), 173–185,

Bury, B., Tiggemann, M. & Slater, A. (2014). Directing gaze: The effect of disclaimer labels on women's visual attention to fashion magazine advertisements. *Body Image, 11* (4), 357–363.

Cash, T. & Smolak, L (Editors, 2012). *Body Image: A Handbook of Science, Practice and Prevention.* Second Edition. Guildford Press.

Cash, T. F. (2004). Body image: Past, present, and future. *Body Image, 1,* 1–5.

Cassone, S. Lewis, V., & Crisp, D.A. (2016). Enhancing positive body image: An evaluation of a cognitive behavioural therapy intervention and an exploration of the role of body shame. *Eating Disorders: The Journal of Treatment and Prevention, 24*(5), 383–392.

Clarke, A., Thompson, A.R., Jenkinson, E., Rumsey, N. & Newell, R. (2014). *CBT for appearance anxiety.* Wiley Blackwell.

Collis, N., Lewis, V., & Crisp, D. (2016). When is Buff Enough? The Effect of Body Attitudes and Narcissistic Traits on Muscle Dysmorphia. *The Journal of Men and Masculinity, 24*(2), 213–225.

Daee, A., Robinson, P., Lawson, M., Turpin, J. A, Gregory, B., & Tobias, J. D. (2002). Psychologic and physiologic effects of dieting in adolescents. *The Southern Medical Journal, 95*(9), 1032–1041.

Darby, A.M., Hay, P.J., Mond, J.M., & Quirk, F. (2011). Community recognition and beliefs about anorexia nervosa and its treatment. *International Journal of Eating Disorders, 45*(1), 120–124.

Darby, A, Hay, P, Mond, J., Quirk, F., Buttner, P., & Kennedy, L. (2009). The rising prevalence of comorbid obesity and eating disorder behaviors from 1995 to 2005. *International Journal of Eating Disorders, 42*(2), 104–108.

Darby, A., Hay, P., Quirk, F., Mond, J., Buettner, P.G., Paxton, S.J., & Kennedy, R.L. (2009). Better psychological health is associated with weight stability in women with eating disorders. *Eating and Weight Disorders, 14*(1), 13–22.

Demir, D., Skouteris, H., Dell-Aquila, D., Aksan, N., McCabe, M. P., Ricciardelli, L.A., Milgrom, J. & Baur, L.A. (2012). An observational approach to testing bi-directional parent–child interactions as influential to child eating and weight, *Early child development and care, 182* (8), 943–950.

Dowds, J. (2010). What do young people think about eating disorders and prevention programmes? Implications for partnerships between health, education and informal youth agencies. *Journal of Public Mental Health, 9*(4), 30–41.

Evans, E.J., Hay, P.J., Mond, J., Paxton, S.J., Quirk, F., Rodgers, B., Jhajj, A.K., & Sawoniewska, M.A. (2011). Barriers to help-seeking in young women with eating disorders: a qualitative exploration in a longitudinal community survey. *Eating Disorders, 19*(3), 270–285.

Fraser, J., Skouteris, H., McCabe, M., Ricciardelli, L.A., Milgrom, J. & Baur, L.A. (2011). Paternal influences on children's weight gain: A systematic review. *Fathering, 9*,(3), 252–267.

Forney, J.K., Hollan, L.A., & Keel, P.K. (2012). Influence of peer context on the relationship between body dissatisfaction and eating pathology in women and men. *International Journal of Eating Disorders, 45*, 982–989.

Fuller-Tyszkiewicz, M., McCabe, M.,. Skouteris, H., Richardson, B., Nihill, K., Watson, B., & Solomon, D. (2015). Does body satisfaction influence self-esteem in adolescents' daily lives? An experience sampling study, *Journal of adolescence, 45*, 11–19.

Gratwick-Sarll, K., Mond, J., & Hay, P. (2013). Self-recognition of eating-disordered behavior in college women: further evidence of poor eating disorders "mental health literacy"? *Eating Disorders, 21*(4), 310–327.

Haines, J., Hannan, P. J., Berg, P. Van Den, & Eisenberg, M. E. (2013). Weight-Related Teasing from Adolescence to Young Adulthood: Longitudinal and Secular Trends between 1999 and 2010. *Obesity, 21*(9), 428–434.

Halliwell, E. & Diedrichs, P. C. (2014). Testing a dissonance body image intervention among young girls. *Health Psychology, 33*(2), 201–204.

Hay, P.J., Buettner, P., Mond, J., Paxton, S.J., Quirk, F., & Rodgers, B. (2012). A community-based study of enduring eating features in young women. *Nutrients, 4*(5), 413–424.

Hay, P., Buttner, P., Mond, J., Paxton, S.J., Rodgers, B., Quirk, F., & Darby, A. (2010). Quality of life, course and predictors of outcomes in community women with EDNOS and common eating disorders. *European Eating Disorders Review, 18*(4), 281–295.

Healthy and active school communities (2004). A resource kit for schools. *Promoting good practice in healthy eating and physical activity for children and youth.* www.healthyactive.gov.au.

Helfert, S., & Warschburger, P. (2011). A prospective study on the impact of peer and parental pressure on body dissatisfaction in adolescent girls and boys. *Body Image, 8*, 101–109.

Katz, I., Keeley, M., Spears, B., Taddeo, C., Swirski, T., & Bates, S. (2014). *Research on youth exposure to, and management of, cyberbullying incidents in Australia*: Synthesis report (SPRC Report 16/2014). Sydney.

Keel, P.K., Forney, K.J., Brown, T.A. & Heatherton, T.F. (2013). Influence of college peers on disordered eating in women and men at 10 year follow up. *Journal of Abnormal Psychology, 122*(1), 105–110.

Kids Matter. (2016). *Building body image at school.* www.kidsmatter.edu.au.

Lantzouni, E., Cox, M.H., Salvator, A., & Crosby, R.D. (2015). Mother–daughter coping and disordered eating. *European Eating Disorders Review, 23*(2), 119–125.

Lewis, V. (2012). *Positive Bodies: Loving the Skin You're In.* Brisbane: Australian Academic Press.

Loth, K.A., Maclehose, R., Bucchianeri, R., Crow, S. & Neumark-Sztainer, O. (2014). Predictors of Dieting and Disordered Eating Behaviors from Adolescence to Young Adulthood. *Journal of Adolescent Health, 55*(5), 705–712.

Makino, M., Tsuboi, K., & Dennerstein, L. (2004). Prevalence of Eating Disorders: A Comparison of Western and Non-Western Countries. *Medscape General Medicine, 6*(3), 49.

McCabe, M.P., Busija, L., Fuller-Tyszkiewicz, M., Ricciardelli, L., Mellor, D. & Mussap, A. (2015). Sociocultural influences on strategies to lose weight, gain weight, and increase muscles among ten cultural groups. *Body Image,* (12),108–114.

McCabe, M.P., Fuller-Tyszkiewicz, M., Mellor, D., Ricciardelli, L., Skouteris, H. & Mussap, A. (2012). Body satisfaction among adolescents in eight different countries. *Journal of Health Psychology, 17*(5), 693–701.

McLean, S.A., Paxton, S.J., Massey, R., Hay, P.J., Mond, J.M., & Rodgers, B. (2014). Stigmatizing attitudes and beliefs about bulimia nervosa: Gender, age, education and income variability in a community sample. *International Journal of Eating Disorders, 47*(4), 353–361.

McPhie, S., Skouteris, H., Fuller-Tyszkiewicz., M., McCabe, M., Ricciardelli, L.A., Milgrom, J., Baur, L.A. & Dell'Aquila, D. (2012), Maternal predictors of preschool child-eating behaviours, food intake and body mass index: A prospective study. *Early Child Development and Care, 182*(8), Special Issue: Parental influences of childhood obesity, 999–1014,

Mellor, D., Hucker, A., Waterhouse, M., binti Mamat, N.H., Xu, X., Cochrane, J., McCabe, M. & Ricciardelli, L. (2014). A cross-cultural study investigating body features associated with male adolescents' body dissatisfaction in Australia, China, and Malaysia. *American Journal of Men's Health, 8*(6), 521–531.

Mitchell, J., Skouteris, H. McCabe, M., Ricciardelli, L.A., Milgrom, J., Baur, L.A., Fuller-Tyszkiewicz, M. & Dwyer, G. (2012). Physical activity in young children: A systematic review of parental influences. *Early Child Development and Care, 182*(11), 1411–1437.

Mitchison, D., Mond, J., Slewa-Younan, S., & Hay, P. (2013). Sex differences in health-related quality of life impairment associated with eating disorder features: A general population study. *International Journal of Eating Disorders, 46*(4), 375–380.

Mitchison, D., Mond, J., Slewa-Younan, S., & Hay, P. (2015). The bidirectional relationship between quality of life and eating disorder symptoms: A 9-year community-based study of Australian women. *PLoS One, 10*(3), 1–18.

Mitchison, D., Hay, P., Slewa-Younan, S., & Mond, J. (2014). The changing demographic profile of eating disorder behaviors in the community. *BMC Public Health, 14*, 1–9.

Mond, J.M., & Baune, B.T. (2009). Overweight, medical comorbidity and health-related quality of life in a community sample of women and men. *Obesity, 17*(8), 1627–1634.

Mond, J.M., & Hay, P.J. (2011). Dissatisfaction versus over-evaluation in a general population sample of women. *International Journal of Eating Disorders, 44*(8), 721–726.

Mond, J., Hall, A., Bentley, C., Harrison, C., Gratwick-Sarll, K., & Lewis, V. (2014). Eating-Disordered Behavior in Adolescent Boys: Eating Disorder Examination Questionnaire (EDE-Q) Norms. *International Journal of Eating Disorders, 47*, 335–341.

Mond, J.M., Hay, P.J., Paxton, S.J., Rodgers, B., Darby, A., Nillson, J., Quirk, F., & Owen, C. (2010). Eating disorders "mental health literacy" in low risk, high risk and symptomatic women: implications for health promotion programs. *Eating Disorders, 18*(4), 267–285.

Mond, J., Mitchison, D., Latner, J., Hay, P., Owen, C., & Rodgers, B. (2013). Quality of life impairment associated with body dissatisfaction in a general population sample of women. *BMC Public Health, 13*(920),,1–11.

National Eating Disorders Collaboration (2016). *Programs and resources available for schools.* www.nedc.com.au.

Neumark-sztainer, D., Bauer, K., & Friend, S. (2010). Family Weight Talk and Dieting : How Much Do They Matter for Body Dissatisfaction and Disordered Eating Behaviors in Adolescent Girls ? *Journal of Adolescent Health, 47*(3), 270–276.

O'Dea, J.A., & O'Dea, J.A. (2005). School-based health education strategies for the improvement of body image and prevention of eating problems: An overview of safe and successful interventions. *Health Education, 105*(1), 11–33.

Paxton, S.J., Wertheim, E.H., Pilawski, A., Durkin, S., & Holt, T. (2002). Evaluations of dieting prevention messages by adolescent girls. *Preventive Medicine, 35*(5), 474–491.

Promoting Health In Schools (2016). *From Evidence to Action.* www.dhhs.tas.gov.au.

Rakhkovkaya, L.M. & Holland, J.M. (2015). Body dissatisfaction in older adults with a disabling health condition. *Journal of Health Psychology.*

Rumsey, N. & Harcourt, D. (2004). Body image and disfigurement: issues and interventions. *Body Image, 1*(1), 83–97.

Rumsey, N. & Harcout, D. (2012). *Oxford Handbook of the Psychology of Appearance.* Oxford University Press.

Rumsey, N. & Harcourt, D. (2005). *The Psychology of Appearance.* Open University Press.

Rutherford, L.M., Brown, J.E., Skouteris, H., Fuller-Tyszkiewicz, M. & Bittman, M. (2015). Screen media, parenting practices, and the family environment in Australia: A longitudinal study of young children's media use, lifestyles, and outcomes for healthy weight. *Journal of Children and Media, 9*(1), 22–39.

Sharpe, H., Naumann, U., & Treasure, J. (2013). Is Fat Talking a Causal Risk Factor for Body Dissatisfaction? A Systematic Review and Meta-Analysis. *International Journal of Eating Disorders, 46*(7), 643–652.

Skouteris, H., McCabe, M., Ricciardelli, L.A., Milgrom, J., Baur, L.A., Aksan, N. & Dell-Aquila, D. (2012). Parent–child interactions and obesity prevention: a systematic review of the literature. *Early Child Development and Care, 182*(2), 153–174.

Tatangelo, G.L. & Ricciardelli, L.A. (2013). A qualitative study of preadolescent boys' and girls' body image: gendered ideals and sociocultural influences, *Body Image, 10*(4), 591–598

The Department of Health. www.health.gov.au. For government reports on the health of Australians.

The Department of Health. www.health.gov.au/pulications. For Government publications on health.

Tiggemann, M. & Slater, A. (2014). Contemporary girlhood: Maternal reports on sexualized behaviour and appearance concern in 4–10 year-old girls. *Body Image, 11*(4), 396–403.

Tiggemann, M. & Slater, A. (2014). NetTweens: The internet and body image concerns in pre-teenage girls. *Journal of Early Adolescence, 34*(5), 606–620.

Tiggemann, M., Slater, A. & Smyth, V. (2014). Retouch free: The effect of labelling media images as not digitally altered on women's body dissatisfaction. *Body Image, 11*(1), 85–88.

Unikel, C., & Ocampo, R. (2012). Disordered Eating and Suicidal Intent: The Role of Thin Ideal Internalisation, Shame and Family Criticism, *European Eating Disorders Review*, 20(1), 39–48.

Williams, R.J. & Ricciardelli, L.A. (2014). Social media and body image concerns: further considerations and broader perspectives, *Sex roles*, 71(11–12), 389–392.

World Health Organisation (2016). www.who.int/en/

World Health Organisation (2016). *Global Strategy On Physical Activity For Health*. http://www.who.int/dietphysicalactivity/factsheet_recommendations/en/

Yager, Z., Diedrichs, P.C., Ricciardelli, L.A. & Halliwell, E. (2013). What works in secondary schools? A systematic review of classroom-based body image programs, *Body Image*, 10(3), 271–281

Yager, Z., & O'Dea, J. (2010). A controlled intervention to promote a healthy body image, reduce eating disorder risk and prevent excessive exercise among trainee health education and physical education teachers. *Health Education Research*, 25(5), 841–852.

APPENDIX

Resources for Children, Young People and Parents Across the Globe

Services in Australia

National

Australian Psychological Society: The professional association of psychologists. For referral to a psychologist in your area. Also, to access tip-sheets and information on evidence-based therapy and assistance in Australia for all mental illnesses and general wellbeing. Website: www.psychology.org.au.

Australian Health Promoting Schools Association: For publications on health promotion in schools. Website: www.ahpsa.org.au.

Beyond Blue: For depression and anxiety support within Australia. Website: Beyondblue.org.au; Phone 1300 22 4636.

Dieticians Association of Australia: For referrals to a nutritionist or dietician. Website: daa.asn.au.

Eating Disorders Victoria: Information and support for people living and caring for those with eating disorders. Website: www.eatingdisorders.org.au.

Headspace, National Youth Mental Health Foundation: A service for young people with mental health concerns with on line talk options and information for children, young people and helpers. Website: Headspace.org.au.

Kids helpline: Phone counselling for children and young people. Phone 1800 55 1800.

Kidsmatter.edu.au: For mental health information.

Lifeline: A crisis support and suicide prevention phone line within Australia. Phone 13 11 14 (24 hours a day).

Men's Line Australia: Support and counselling for men. Phone: 1300 78 99 78 (24 hours) Website: www.mensline. org.au.

Nutrition Society of Australia: For information on nutrition and services in Australia. Website: www.nsa.asn.au.

Nutrition Australia: For information on nutrition and services in Australia. Website: www.nutritionaustralia.org.

Parent line: Help for young people and parents within Australia. Phone 1300 30 1300. Website: www.parent-line.com.au.

Reachout.com Australia: For information about body image, wellbeing and mental illness in youth.

The Butterfly Foundation: Foundation for eating disorders and support for Australians experiencing eating disorders. Website: thebutterflyfoundation.org.au.

Wesley Hospital: For the treatment of eating disorders. Website: www.wesleymission.org.au.

AUSTRALIAN STATES AND TERRITORIES

Australian Capital Territory

ACT Eating Disorders Program: A specialist, community-based, multidisciplinary team providing assessment and treatment programs for people with eating disorders.

Consultation/liaison is also available for health professionals. Phone (02) 6205 1519 or 1 800 621 354 for 24 hours Crisis Team. Website: www.health.act.gov.au.

Mental Health, ACT Health: Crisis help 1800 629 354 (24 hours). Access to child and adult mental health services. Website: www.health.act.gov.au.

Mental Illness ACT: Educates the Canberra community about mental illness. It aims to reduce stigma and discrimination, improve knowledge, and to raise awareness about the importance of getting help early. They speak in schools. Website: www.mieact.org.au.

Victoria

Eating Disorders Foundation of Victoria: A non-profit organisation which supports those affected by eating disorders and aims to better inform the community about disordered eating. Phone (03) 9885 0318. Non-metro Victorian callers call 1300 550 236 (helpline). Website: www.eatingdisorders.org.au. Email: edfv@eatingdisorders.org.au.

Mental Illness fellowship: Help for individuals and families living with mental illness. Phone: +61 03 8486 4200. enquiries@mifellowship.org. Helpline: 03 8486 4222.

New South Wales

The Butterfly Foundation: The Butterfly Foundation is dedicated to bring change to culture, policy and practice in the prevention, treatment and support of those affected by eating disorders and negative body image. It has a telephone helpline for people with eating disorders and their family and friends. Support is also available via email. Phone 1800 33 4673. Website: www.thebutterflyfoundation.org.au.   Email: support@thebutterflyfoundation.org.au.

Queensland

Eating Disorders Association Inc: A non-profit organisation that provides information, support and referral services. Phone (07) 3394 3661. Website: www.eda.org.au. Email: admin@eda.org.au.

South Australia

Aceda: A not for profit community organisation to support people with eating disorders. Phone (08) 8297 4088. Website: www.aceda.org.au. Email: aceda@aceda.org.au.

Western Australia

ARAFMI Mental Health Carers & Friends Association Inc: A non-profit community based organisation that provides information and support for families and friends of people with mental health issues, including: Family support counselling, support group program advocacy, respite and community education. Phone (08) 9427 7100 or 1800 811 747 (rural freecall). Website: www.arafmi.asn.au.

Centre for Clinical Intervention: A free, specialist, state-wide mental health program offering cognitive behavioural therapy for people with eating disorders, as well as other mental health conditions. Phone (08) 9227 6003. Website: www.cci.health.wa.gov.au. Email: info.cci@health.wa. gov.au.

Women's Health Works: A non-profit community organisation that provides a range of education, information and support services to women, including self-help groups for people experiencing an eating disorder. Phone (08) 9300 1566. website: www.womenshealthworks.org.au. Email: info@womenshealthworks.org.au.

Tasmania

Tasmanian Eating Disorders Website: This site provides online information and resources for people with eating disorders and support groups for sufferers and carers. Phone (03) 6222 7222. Website: www.tas.eatingdisorders.org.au. Email: tas.eatingdisorders@dhhs.tas.gov.au.

Services in New Zealand

Eating Difficulties Education Network: A non-profit community agency based in Auckland, Aotearoa New Zealand. Phone (09) 378 9039. Website: www.eden.org.nz. Email: info@eden.org.nz.

Helplines: The Depression Helpline (0800 111 757); Healthline (0800 611 116); Lifeline (0800 543 354); Samaritans (0800 726 666); Youthline (0800 376 633); Alcohol Drug Helpline (0800 787 797).

Ministry of Health: For information about mental health services in New Zealand. www.health.govt.nz.

New Zealand Psychologists Board: For information about psychologists in New Zealand. http://www.psychologistsboard.org.nz/.

Services in The United Kingdom

Anorexia & Bulimia Care: National charity offering helplines, 1:2:1 befriending support, and nutrition guidance. Website: www.anorexiabulimiacare.org.uk.

Beat: Beating eating disorders, a support service for professionals and the general public. Website: www.b-eat.co.uk Helpline 0345 634 1414. Youthline 0345 634 7650.

British Association for Counselling and Psychotherapy: To find professionals who specialise in treating eating disorders and other mental health issues. Website: www.itsgoodtotalk.org.uk.

British Psychological Society: The professional association of psychologists. For referral to a psychologist. Also, to access tip-sheets and information on evidence-based therapy and assistance in the UK. Website: www.bps.org.uk.

Counselling Directory: To find professionals who specialise in treating eating disorders and other mental health issues. Website: www.counselling-directory.org.uk.

Men get EDs too: Info, helplines and support groups for male sufferers and their families Website: www.mengeted-stoo.co.uk.

National Centre for Eating Disorders: Offers help for sufferers and training for professionals. http://eating-disorders.org.uk/.

NHS Choices: Explore the sections in the Health A-Z on eating disorders and their treatments, and the Live Well section. Website: www.nhs.uk.

Overeaters Anonymous: National support group meetings based on the AA 12 step recovery approach. Website: www.oagb.org.uk.

Royal College of Psychiatrists: Very readable leaflets on a variety of topics on eating disorders including help for teachers, parents and children. Website: www.rcpsych.ac.uk. http://www.rcpsych.ac.uk/healthadvice/parentsandyouthinfo/parentscarers/eatingdisorders.aspx.

The Centre for Appearance Research: Conducts research and assists people living with appearance related concerns. It is part of the University of the West of England. Website: www1.uwe.ac.uk.

The National Centre for Eating Disorders: To find professionals who specialise in treating eating disorders and other mental health issues. Website: www.eating-disorders.org.uk.

Services in The United States

American Psychological Association: To find psychologists in your area as well as tips for management of mental health and services available across America. Website: www.apa.org.

American Suicide Hotline: Numerous helplines for a range of mental illness help. National Suicide Prevention Lifeline 1800 273 8255. Website: wwwcrisistextline.org where you can text your concern.

Eating Disorder Treatment Centres: Use this website to find eating disorder treatment centres around the USA. http://www.eatingdisorderhope.com/treatment-centers.

National Eating Disorders Association: It supports individuals and families affected by eating disorders. Website: www.nationaleatingdisorders.org.

National Institute of Mental Health: Help for all mental illnesses. Call the toll-free, 24-hour hotline of the National Suicide Prevention Lifeline at 1-800-273-TALK (1-800-273-8255) to be connected to a trained counsellor at a suicide crisis centre nearest you. Website: www.nimh.nih.gov.

National Suicide Prevention Lifeline. For help for yourself or someone close. Call 1800 273 8255. Website: www.sucide-preventionlifeline.org.

The Alliance For Eating Disorder Awareness: Helps support those with eating disorders and those recovering. Website: www.allianceforeatingdisorders.com.

Women's Health: Office on Women's Health US Department of Health and Human Services. Website: www.women-shealth.gov.

Services in Canada

Canada Suicide Hotlines: For crisis help in your area. Website: www.suicde.org/hotlines.

Canadian Women's Health Network: Helps women and girls with general wellbeing. Website: www.cwhn.ca.

Eating Disorder Hope: Canadian eating disorder treatment information and resources. Website: www.eatingdisorder-hope.com.

National Eating Disorder Information Centre: provides resources on eating disorders and weight preoccupation. Website: www.nedic.ca.